Music Distribution and the Internet

To my family, my wife Fadime and daughter Melike-Grace

Music Distribution and the Internet

A Legal Guide for the Music Business

ANDREW SPARROW

GOWER

Published by
Gower Publishing Limited
Gower House
Croft Road
Aldershot
Hampshire GU11 3HR
England

Gower Publishing Company
Suite 420
101 Cherry Street
Burlington, VT 05401-4405
USA

British Library Cataloguing in Publication Data
Sparrow, Andrew Peter
  Music distribution and the Internet : a legal guide for the
  music business
  1. Music trade - Law and legislation 2. Internet - Law and
  legislation 3. Music - Computer network resources
  4. Copyright - Music
  I. Title
  343'.07878

  ISBN-10: 0 566 08709 X

Library of Congress Control Number: 2006929151

Printed and bound in Great Britain by MPG Books Ltd. Bodmin, Cornwall.

Contents

CHAPTER 1

Introduction to the Internet and its Impact on Music Distribution

In 2004 there was a series of events to celebrate ten years of the Internet as a commercial medium. In a decade, a communications revolution had penetrated the day-to-day operations of companies all over the world and afforded individuals access to information on a scale unimaginable a few years earlier. There are now close to a billion people on the Internet. The Internet of course had not been conceived with business in mind and it took some considerable time for its potential to be identified even following the development of the World Wide Web. However, its time came and with it wholly misplaced forecasts for its immediate commercial impact.

In the mid 1990s most people had never heard of the Internet and certainly businesses could not establish with any degree of certainty how it might erode or enhance their marketplace. So arose the rapid Internet ascendancy in the minds of consumers and business alike and, within a time frame which can be measured in weeks, the inevitable fall in fortune of its early proponents. The unrealized commercial promise of the medium caused many to dismiss the Internet as having no future in the sphere of international commerce. Whilst in large part at that time the view was justified it made no allowance for the fact that in the history of all commercial innovations that succeed there was once a time when they did not.

The technology continued to evolve. Gradually people began to revisit the medium in more measured terms and make their first Internet purchase, or book their first flight online. The advent of broadband offering hugely improved download time paved the way for the delivery of content via the Internet which would appeal to consumers and thus renewed enthusiasm on the part of those who would provide web-based services. In the last decade a number of now household names have proved the efficacy of the Internet for business. Amazon spawned a revolution in book retailing and created a panacea for consumer purchases of books, DVDs and CDs, which others have since followed. EasyJet led the use of the Internet for flight reservations, and through the cost savings achieved by use of the Web also developed the low-cost airline model now a part of the commercial aviation industry. In 2005 Google is the highest-valued media company in the world. Yahoo has around 400 million users per month. To say that the Internet has changed our way of life is an understatement.

In all this time it was recognized that if e-commerce in its broadest sense did become a feature of business then there would have to be sensible legal governance. Both commerce and consumers would require a set of rules which defined their rights in the online environment. Whilst the fortunes of the Internet's commercial career fluctuated, the legal issues surrounding Internet business were always founded on a genuine need to safeguard the interests of a future online community.

Even in the closing months of the last century there was little law which had been conceived with the Internet in mind. For the most part, lawyers were compelled to shoehorn legal principles having their origins a further one hundred years in the past into the new medium. From concluding a legally binding contract online to upholding individual privacy rights, lawmakers struggled with the concept of the Internet. However, new rules did find their way on to the statute books and most of these have their origins in the European Union in the form of Regulations and Directives. As such they provide a panacea for legal treatment of e-commerce which governs the now 25 member states of the EU.

One major arena where the Internet would find a home is music distribution. Digital technology enables information, software, text, pictures and, importantly, music, to be copied millions of times without the loss of quality, downloaded without the knowledge of the copyright holder and transmitted around the world instantly over networks. It was clear that traditional models for music distribution were about to be overturned.

Whilst the issue of copyright and the rights of music artists and record companies alike have caught the attention of the media in recent years the extent of legal control for the music industry in general for online activity is far wider than most would appreciate. Protecting intellectual property in musical works is just one of a myriad of laws which to a varying degree impact on media distribution using the Internet.

In short, there is hardly an aspect of Internet music promotion, sale and distribution which does not have a legal dimension. This book is intended to provide those connected with the music industry an insight into the legal requirements they must meet as they embrace the erstwhile enemy. We will examine how contracts with consumers over the Internet must be concluded and consider the various legal terms and conditions which should govern the sale of physical product to online music buyers. Issues surrounding how website users' personal information needs to be handled will be reviewed together with the rules which prescribe how that data can be used for ongoing marketing of artists' work and merchandise. The latest copyright protection laws as they apply to the Internet will be assessed and some strategic agreements with other parties in the online channel are looked at to see the kind of issues which need to be addressed. It will be seen that in the context of a typical music company website selling CDs and offering other music-based services for example, no less than nine different pieces of legislation must be adhered to in the legal terms and conditions on the site.

The problem facing lawmakers in the digital era is the sheer pace of development. The dynamics of the technology are changing so rapidly. This presents difficulties because whilst it is recognized that the Internet will continue to advance, one cannot be certain of the direction the new media industry is heading and which products will become widespread. Just as iPod equipment dominates the market, record companies are now investing in digital formats such as full-track mobile phone downloads. Forecasts predict that half of all mobile users in Europe will subscribe to a 3G service by 2010. The opportunity for the music industry to offer music and video promotion direct to mobile users is clear. Attempting to make new laws future-proof is not an easy undertaking. The issue of delivery mechanism for content is significant to how the law governs in ways not immediately apparent. When television was broadcast by terrestrial means, when radio was transmitted over the airwaves and print media had its own clearly defined domain, legal concepts for controlling content were easier to grasp. The Internet upset traditional models. With increased convergence of media and technology, music and film can be delivered to your mobile phone. Television, or rather audio-visual content, can be viewed at the time of the viewer's choosing and geographical borders become meaningless.

It should be pointed out that the law relating to Internet music distribution is complex. Drawing together the various strands of each new law to explain how those in the music industry can go about using the Internet actually brings into play many different legal principles albeit all directed at the medium. It will also be seen that the majority of the law in this field has been introduced in 2004 and 2005. It is the way of legal development that legislation must be interpreted to establish how it impacts on specific facts. This is the preserve of case law. Given the short time since introduction of the legislation there is very little case law precedent at the time of writing but undoubtedly this will develop in the coming years.

The book is written for those in the music industry or associated with it. Whether they be record companies, music publishers, artist managers, composers and songwriters or lawyers wishing to gain an insight into the subject, all should find the work useful. Practical advice is given on how to approach key relationships with the Internet music-buying consumer and other online media providers. The law is explained in straightforward terms and applied throughout in a music business context. It is hoped that the reader will gain a good understanding of the legal issues in this field and an appreciation not otherwise easily gained of the all-pervading nature of the law in the rapidly expanding, constantly evolving and fascinating arena that is new media.

CHAPTER 2

Online Contracts for the Sale of Music and Merchandise

Music retailers and record industry suppliers may have been slow to adapt to the world of Internet music but at the time of writing, the music industry is now quickly taking advantage of the flexibility and low scale-up costs of digital music. Music retailers which once only sold music that they had delivered to their stores have the capability of becoming record distributors. Music businesses wishing to increase participation with their artists' fans have adopted the Internet and mobile phones for fans to win prizes and speak to other fans. Interactive media generates revenue and increases loyalty for the artists' and the music business.

There is a transformation in the way in which people interact with music. Those with broadband connections use the Internet more than they watch television, while young people familiar with sophisticated mobile phones are much more receptive to watching television on the phone. New services present new market opportunities for the music business.

Nonetheless, whatever format is used, to transact business over the Internet requires the formation of legally binding contracts. The issue of how a contract comes into existence when dealing online is one which from the first stirrings of e-commerce caused significant legal attention. There had to be an ability for website operators and their visitors to enter into binding legal relations. However, it was also clear that the very nature of the Internet would present a raft of new legal problems. Which country's law would apply to this global medium? At what point would a contract come into existence? These questions were resolved and are reviewed in this book. However, to understand how a music business can operate safely online it is necessary to consider how English law approaches the matter of contract formation generally. This is because these long-established legal principles apply to Internet trade and shape the way which websites must be configured. In this section we will examine these contract law considerations and see how a contract can be made over the Internet and by mobile phone text messaging.

The assertion by Bill Gates in his book *The Road Ahead* that the Internet 'will carry us into a new world of low-friction, low-overhead capitalism, in which market information will be plentiful and transaction costs low' has proved correct. It is this characteristic which has exercised the minds of those in the music industry. The access to online music files is limitless and vast databases can be maintained of music works. The tracks can be distributed without the need for physical dispatch, thus making transactions costs almost non-existent.

The Internet represents a triumph of technology over the bonds which hitherto prevented instantaneous communication on a truly global scale.

As the medium thus fits within an established legal framework, so it is necessary to understand the process of contract formation. Such an appreciation is critical to online business as the sheer openness of the system can cause problems.

ENGLISH CONTRACT LAW

English law requires a number of things to happen before a legally binding contract can be said to have been formed. A contract is founded on agreement. In its purest form agreement arises from offer and acceptance. One person makes an offer, another person accepts that offer. However the law demands four elements to constitute a legally enforceable contract. They are:

- offer

- acceptance

- consideration (usually payment)

- an intention to create legal relations.

In this chapter we will only consider the concept of an offer, and another important issue for proper contract formation – that of the capacity of those under 18 to enter into contracts.

OFFER

An *offer* is a proposition put by one person (or persons) to another person (or persons) coupled by an intimation that they are willing to be bound to that proposition. The *offeror*, that is, the person who makes the offer, may make an offer to a particular person, or to a group of persons or, as in the context of the Internet, the entire world.

This offer may be made in writing, or in spoken words or by conduct. The first two can be grasped immediately and often the written contract takes the form of an elaborate document with numerous clauses and sub-clauses. How can conduct create an offer? Well, an everyday act of conduct which constitutes an offer can be found in a bus driver pulling up at a bus stop.

The intimation that the offeror is willing to be bound need not be stated in words, be they written or spoken. It may be, and frequently is, inferred from the nature of the offeror's proposition or from the circumstances from which the proposition is made.

When you make an offer, you are expressing a desire to enter into a contract based on specified terms and conditions on the understanding that if the other party accepts it, the agreement will be legally binding.

Offers can be made using virtually any form of communication. Over the years, as new means of communication developed, the courts had to establish how contracts were to be formed by the use of developing mediums – from simple letter post, to the advent of the telephone, fax machine and now by email, SMS (short message service) text and of course over the Internet.

It is vital to consider this legal explanation of what constitutes an 'offer'. English law states that if a reasonable person would interpret a particular action or communication as an offer (a readiness to bind oneself), it is an offer whether the party intended it or not.

It is therefore the appearance of an offer which is more important than actual intent. It can be seen that this is where the danger to electronic business exists. Careless online statements or poorly constructed websites could amount to a music business making unintentional offers to the world which could result in unwanted binding legal contracts once consumers accept.

OFFER DISTINGUISHED FROM INVITATION TO TREAT

There is a concept in English contract law which at first hearing sounds odd but which is necessary in the sales environment and is actually central to website commercial dealings. It is necessary to distinguish a true offer from an *invitation to treat*. The importance of the distinction is that if a true offer is made and is then accepted the offeror is bound.

Conversely, if what the offeror said or did is not a true offer, but merely an invitation to treat, the other person cannot by saying 'I accept' bind the offeror and thus create a contract. Important though this distinction is, it is not always easy to make it.

The contrast between the two principles can best be illustrated by the use of examples common to commercial life. First, the tender situation where the distinction between an offer and an invitation to treat is reasonably clearly seen. If a company asks a number of suppliers to put in tenders for supplying it with some particular goods or services, the company is not, thereby, making an offer to those suppliers.

Consequently, the company is not bound to accept the lowest or any other tender. It is not the company which makes the offer: the offer comes from the supplier in the form of a tender or estimate.

The next example of an invitation to treat is the display of articles on shelves in a shop. The offer is not made by the shop owner. They are only making an invitation to treat. The offer is in fact made by the customer taking the article to the cash desk and tendering money to purchase. That offer by the customer can then be accepted or refused by the shop. The courts take the same view of goods displayed in a shop window.

The same rule applies to an advertisement placed, for example, by a company stating that it is willing to sell some goods. The general rule is that an advertisement is not an offer, merely an invitation to treat. We consider advertisements in the context of the Internet in Chapter 12.

For the online music business to protect itself from making unintentional offers, it needs to observe the fine distinction between an offer and an invitation.

The Internet uses modern digital technology and ordinary telephone lines. It is not a closed system like telex and it offers much more through its interconnecting networks. Anyone with a modern computer, a modem, suitable programs and a paid-up subscription to one of the Internet service providers (ISPs), can gain access to the system. By means of that system, a user can obtain information from websites, send messages through email, and order merchandise and services.

A contract need not be a detailed formal document. It is possible to form a legally recognized contract by the simple exchange of email. There might be arguments over uncertainty of terms and perhaps the court may refuse to confirm a contract if there are so many aspects of the purported agreement unclear to make the contract void for uncertainty. Nonetheless, email exchange can create legal relations so care must be taken. A contract can also be formed by mobile phone SMS. An exchange of text messages could constitute a contract between the parties.

MUSIC WEBSITES

A website operated by a music business is the electronic equivalent of a shop window. Email price lists for merchandise for example are similarly analogous to circulars in conventional commerce. The better view is that a website constitutes an invitation to treat by its form rather than an offer for sale. However there is no legal certainty.

It is important the music business makes it clear that its website does not constitute an irrevocable offer for sale of the music made available or the merchandise or services detailed on the site. To minimize the risk, the music website and electronic mail solicitations should have disclaimers explicitly defining them to be invitations to treat, and not offers.

Consider that if the content of the music business website constitutes an offer then the business will have no control over who it becomes legally bound to. This would be a commercially intolerable scenario. By the inclusion of an appropriate disclaimer it will ensure that it has the ability to select customers or clients and manage its supply of music, merchandise or services.

For many reasons the music business may not wish to deal with all consumers from all jurisdictions across the world. The website may be targeted to specific audiences and it is common for record companies to operate various websites if the company is international, perhaps with one site covering Europe and another governing the US market. Thus, it is important for a music business to retain the power to accept or refuse. In this way it can decline online customers without the fear of being in breach of contract.

In fact if the music business only ever intends to accept orders from say UK-based record-buying consumers, because the Internet is a global medium, it must place a notice on its website stating that the contents of its website are for UK customers only.

DISCLAIMERS AND EXEMPTION CLAUSES

We are all familiar with clauses in contracts which seek to restrict or limit a company's legal liability in certain situations. A *disclaimer* or *exemption clause* is a term in a contract which seeks to exempt one of the parties from liability in certain events. The same principles apply to what are called limitation clauses. These are clauses which attempt to limit, rather than wholly exclude, a party's liability. An example is a clause which states that complaints must be made within a certain period of time.

An exemption clause is a perfectly legitimate device in contracts between parties of equal bargaining power. In general the courts will regard two businesses which wish to enter into a contract as having equal bargaining power. Clearly, there are in reality significant differences in commercial strength between businesses and many commercial dealings are entered into on terms favourable to the stronger party. That is simple commercial reality. Broadly though, the law treats both businesses as having a greater understanding of commercial transactions than, say, the individual consumer.

Where the parties are unequal, exclusion clauses may work unjustly. The law will regard a business and a consumer as unequal parties – the business treated as the dominant party. In this country, as indeed throughout the EU, consumers are afforded considerable protection when dealing with businesses. It is that policy which dictates much of the law relating to online sales to consumers and which we consider in this book in a variety of contexts.

Online consumer trade has seen huge growth in recent years, particularly for items such as flight bookings, hotel bookings, and book, CD and DVD purchases. The acquisition of music, of course, via the Internet has also found its market.

In respect of online contracts made under English law and in particular contracts made with consumers, the music business as supplier of merchandise or services will need to take into account the provisions of various relevant statutes.

As stated, the law assumes that consumers deserve greater legal protection. Clearly, this distinction is relevant in the online and mobile environment. It is essential the music business appreciates who its website is targeted towards, as this will determine the nature and extent of the online legal terms and conditions it may post on its website. We examine some examples of online terms and conditions in Chapter 3.

A number of Acts of Parliament and Regulations have developed which find their basis in EU Directives designed to give the consumer protection. It is useful to consider these briefly.

Consumer Credit Act 1974

This Act regulates the content of agreements for the provision or credit, sets out various procedures which must be followed to protect consumers and establishes a regime for licensing businesses which provide consumer credit or consumer hire. As a result of changes made to the legislation the provision of consumer credit online to UK consumers is now permitted.

Consumer Protection Act 1987

In certain circumstances this Act imposes strict liability on the manufacturer (and others in the distribution chain) of defective goods which cause death or personal injury or loss or damage to property.

Unfair Terms in Consumer Contracts Regulations 1994

These Regulations came into force on 1 July 1995. They give effect to a European Community Directive (93/13/EEC) to promote harmonization of the laws of member states so as to ensure that contracts with consumers do not include terms which are unfair to the consumer. They apply to standard contracts entered into between the sellers or suppliers of goods or services to consumers. They introduce a general concept of *unfairness* in terms. If such terms are unfair then by Regulation 5(1) 'they shall not be binding on the consumer'. The definition of a *consumer* under the Regulations is quite wide. Regulation 2(1) defines a consumer as a 'natural person who, in making a contract to which these Regulations apply, is acting for purposes which are outside his business.' This definition includes persons running small businesses for activities which are incidental to their business.

Unfair Contract Terms Act 1977 (as amended) (UCTA)

This is the Act which dominates exclusion and limitation clauses and how they are to be regarded at law. The Act applies to music business legal terms imposed on consumers. It also applies to Internet sales of music and merchandise online.

It is first necessary to study two definitions in the Act: first, *business liability* and second, *deals as consumer*. Most of the Act applies only to business liability and the consumer has a specially favoured status under the legislation.

Business liability is liability arising from things done by a person in the course of business or from the occupation of business premises. A person deals as consumer if they do not make the contract in the course of a business and the other party does make the contract in the course of a business. If the contract is for the supply of goods, there is an additional point, namely that the goods must be of a type ordinarily supplied for private use or consumption.

Business liability for death or personal injury resulting from negligence cannot be excluded or restricted by any contract term or notice.

In the case of other loss or damage, a music business cannot so exclude or restrict its business liability for negligence except insofar as the terms or notice satisfies the requirement of reasonableness.

The requirement of reasonableness is that the term shall be a fair and reasonable one to be included having regard to all the circumstances which were, or ought to have been, known to or in the contemplation of the parties when the contract was made.

The Act lays down guidelines for the application of the reasonableness test. So when one party deals as consumer or on the music business's standard written terms of business, the music business cannot:

- when it is in breach of contract exclude or restrict its business liability in respect of the breach;

- claim to be entitled to render a contractual performance substantially different from that which was reasonably expected of it;

- claim to be entitled to render no performance at all except in all three cases subject to the requirement of reasonableness.

It is important to appreciate that the Act does not set out a generalized prohibition of exemption clauses or a generalized requirement of reasonableness. There are many contracts to which it does not apply or does not fully apply. These include contracts of insurance and contracts relating to transfer of land.

CAPACITY

In the English law of contract, people below the age of majority, which is 18, are called minors. The law is based on two principles. The first is that the law must protect minors against their inexperience, which may enable an adult to take unfair advantage of them or to induce them to enter into a contract which is improvident. This principle is based on the general rule that minors are not bound by their contracts. The second principle is that the law should not cause unnecessary hardship to adults who deal fairly with minors. Under this principle certain contracts with minors are valid.

It is beyond the scope of this book to examine the various situations where contracts can be upheld against minors as we are only concerned with the online world as it applies to Internet use.

A useful example of how the problem of contracting with children can arise in the context of the Internet and mobile communications lies in the 'Crazy Frog' ringtone. A company called Jamster sells ringtones. In 2005 it flooded television commercial breaks with adverts which featured an animated amphibian in a leather motorcycle cap and goggles. The character was supported by an annoying music accompaniment. The advertising campaign was hugely successful and the music track topped the UK charts, and sales of the ringtones version also represented a major commercial success. The Advertising Standards Authority received several complaints about the campaign but the real cause for concern lay in the alleged misleading promotion of the ringtone. This led to complaints being laid before the Independent Committee for the Supervision of Standards of Telephone Information Services (ICSTIS). It received over 100 complaints from people who thought they had bought the ringtone at a price of £3 only to find that they had also unwittingly signed up for a subscription service costing £3 per week. Many of the subscribers were children and the error was only discovered when parents received their phone bill.

CHECKLIST

- Ensure by including in the website terms and conditions that the existence of the music website is expressed to be an invitation to treat and not an offer for sale of the items made available through it.

- Only include exclusion or limitation clauses in online contract terms which are reasonable whether dealing with consumers or other businesses.

- Exercise caution if targeting the online service to young people and be mindful of the legal capacity laws.

CHAPTER 3

Website Terms and Conditions

SUPPLY OF MUSIC CDS AND OTHER MERCHANDISE OVER THE INTERNET

HOW TO ENSURE LEGAL TERMS GOVERN THE CONTRACT

In this section we will review the principal terms and conditions which should operate to govern the online sale of physical product typically offered by music companies and associated businesses over the Internet. This might include the sale of promotional material. As throughout this book, we will refer to the term *music business* which might be a record company, publishing company, music retailer or any other business associated with the promotion, retail or distribution of musical content. For convenience of description we will simply use this generic term.

Elsewhere in this book we examine the huge importance of marketing an artist and the merchandise that surrounds the artist. Record company websites have grown in sophistication in recent years as has the range of services they typically offer. The more successful an artist is, the more likely that fans will want to buy products which provide more information about them. They will buy products which bear the artist's likeness such as calendars, posters, screensavers and clothing items. They will also want to purchase products the artist is associated with such as food, drinks and sweets. Consumers generally are spending more than ever online and so the Internet is a vital tool for music businesses.

The manner in which merchandise must be made available to website visitors is prescribed by a variety of laws which many music businesses may not appreciate.

We have seen in Chapter 2 the important legal distinction between an offer and an invitation to treat and why it is so vital to a music business operating a website which sells merchandise.

There are many legislative requirements of websites in terms of the information they must display. The full extent of these depends upon the range of services the website provides. Usually the music business would not simply sell CDs. The company would want to supply information about bands, venues for concerts, possibly offer ticket purchase facilities and produce an online magazine. (The legal terms for online magazine subscriptions are reviewed in Chapter 11.) Certainly the company would want to gather information from its record-buying online consumers, and it is highly likely that the website will utilize and display the intellectual property of artists, the music business and third parties. Thus, for a website of reasonable sophistication, providing a good range of content for music fans, there may well be nine separate pieces of legislation which must be complied with before the website can meet its full responsibilities. These include obligations under the Electronic Commerce Regulations 2002 (Chapter 4), the Data Protection Act 1998 (Chapter 7), the Privacy and Electronic Communications Regulations 2002 (Chapter 6), the Consumer Protection (Contracts Concluded by Means of Distance Communication) Regulations 2000 (Chapter 8), the Unfair Contract Terms Act 1977 (Chapter 2), the Unfair Terms in Consumer Contracts Regulations 1999, the Sale of Goods Act 1979, the Supply of Goods and Services Act 1982, the Disability Discrimination Act 1995 (Chapter 14) and various case law.

EXAMPLE CLAUSES FOR THE SUPPLY OF MERCHANDISE AND SERVICES ONLINE

The following review of the issues a music business should cover in its website legal terms and conditions addresses the above legal necessities and also those matters which are commercially desirable for the online music retailer in its dealings with consumer website purchasers.

As discussed earlier, the website terms and conditions must be brought to the attention of the user before the contract is concluded in order for those terms to be validly incorporated into the contract. Under English law the most effective way this can be achieved is to require the visitor to click through the terms before being able to proceed further in the online ordering process. This is known as a *click-wrap* contract and the proper place for the display of the terms is at the point prior to the checkout facility in the online basket which is now familiar to all web users. The terms can also govern the sale if reasonable steps have been taken to bring them to the attention of the online consumer before the contract is entered into. It is unclear just how that might occur but it is not safe to build a hyperlink on the website to the legal terms where that hyperlink appears at the bottom of a webpage requiring the visitor to scroll down to the page in order to even see the terms.[1]

There is some uncertainty in the context of mobile access to Internet music websites. For example, if the music business wishes to market to its consumer base via their mobile telephones there are clear rules it must follow. We consider in Chapter 6 how the company must go about targeting and notifying those phone subscribers. If the web content produced by the music business contains an offer for example to buy a CD single at discounted rates, the limitation in screen size of the mobile apparatus will almost certainly prevent the display on the page of full terms and conditions. Therefore the company might refer to the full terms in a prominent part of the webpage used by mobile phone visitors. Those terms might then be displayed on a website and the URL for that site listed in the mobile invitation. Whilst this is the only practical way to address the problem of notification of terms, one can see the difficulties it presents.

The opening paragraphs of the website terms and conditions should request that the visitor carefully reads the terms and that by clicking the 'I Accept' button, usually appearing at the bottom of the terms, the visitor agrees to be bound by the terms. The steps necessary for the visitor to conclude the contract must be set out as required by the E-Commerce Regulations 2002 (Chapter 4). It would be prudent for the music business to make clear that any delivery dates stated in the website are estimates only and no liability will ensue for late delivery.

Every attempt must be made by the business to ensure prices are correct but usually the company will insert a provision confirming that the order must be validated by it as part of the acceptance procedure. That way, if the actual price of the article differs from that displayed on the website, the discrepancy can be picked up by the music business. It can then notify the purchaser of the correct price and the purchaser can then decide whether to cancel the order or proceed.

As we have seen there is a very good reason why a website must be characterized as an invitation to treat from a legal perspective. To reinforce this status it is important to insert a provision in the terms that the music business is entitled to refuse any order placed by its online consumer. If the order is accepted then the company should state that it will confirm acceptance

---

1   US case *Specht* v *Netscape Communications Corp*, 150 F Supp 2d 585 (SDNY 5 July 2001).

by electronic means, which is usually to the email address the consumer has indicated on registration or ordering. The music business should then specify a date by which the order will be fulfilled and perhaps a backstop date in the absence of a specified date.

Although more a commercial matter the company might want to consider the supply of alternative merchandise if the product ordered by the online consumer is not available. This will depend on the type of product to be supplied via the website and it is really a matter of how the company wishes to meet customer expectations. If it does want this flexibility then it should insert a clause in its terms to allow for supply of alternative products.

We now turn to the issue of return of merchandise which has been ordered from a music website. We will consider in Chapter 8 the requirements of the Consumer Protection (Contracts Concluded by Means of Distance Communication) Regulations 2000. It will be recalled that the online customer must be told their rights under those Regulations. The place to do this and to set out comprehensively the company's returns policy is in the legal terms on its website.

The company should state that the consumer has seven days in which to return any merchandise they have purchased and this includes if the customer simply changes their minds.[2] The customer must be instructed to notify the company in writing, which can of course include email, within those seven days. The company must then refund the customer as soon as possible. However, it is open to the music business to require the customer to be responsible for the costs of return post and packaging. If this is the case then it must be specified in the terms – it will not be implied by the courts. Clearly, the customer is under an obligation to keep the merchandise in good condition in the meantime and this must be pointed out to them.

It is useful at this juncture to remind the reader that this consumer right to return goods without question only applies to Internet sales in the EU, and there are a number of exclusions. In the example website terms we are considering in this section we have assumed that the music website is supplying products such as music CDs, DVDs and other physical merchandise. In each of these cases the online consumer has the benefit of the Distance Selling Regulations. However, if the music website also offers deals such as accommodation and ticket sales, in other words where the services are to be supplied on a particular date or specific period, then the Regulations will not apply. In such cases the

---

2   Consumer Protection (Distance Selling) DS Regulations 2000 (SI 2000/2334).

consumer does not have the right to a cancellation period of seven days. The other exception is the making available of online music for download against payment. In this instance as we have seen, the music buyer cannot demand a refund or cancel the contract since the benefit has already been obtained. It may be seen that a music website can become difficult to properly place in the legal environment which governs online sales. Some products available from the website allows the consumer return rights; other items may not. It is important to take advice from a lawyer with an understanding of Internet issues to ensure that whatever terms the company wishes to incorporate in its website are properly drafted.

The other aspect in relation to returns brings into play long-established consumer legislation. The law implies certain warranties into consumer contracts whether they be for the sale of goods or for the provision of services. So for example, the goods supplied must match their description[3] and the goods must be of satisfactory quality.[4] This includes their state and condition, their fitness for purpose, appearance and finish, safety, durability and freedom from minor defects. In addition, the law implies a warranty that the goods are fit for a particular purpose if the seller knows that purpose, except where the circumstances show that the buyer did not rely, or it was unreasonable for the buyer to rely, on the skill or judgement of the seller.[5] All these matters are implied by law into Internet sales of merchandise supplied by music companies to consumers they cannot be excluded to any extent under the Unfair Contract Terms Act 1977. Even if the provisions were not included in the legal terms governing the website the online consumer would benefit from their effect. Clearly, it is desirable to address the implied warranties in the terms since as we can see, a variety of other legal requirements need to be incorporated.

However, where the Internet music company is supplying goods to another business the position differs. The Unfair Contract Terms Act 1977 allows for the foregoing implied warranties to be limited or indeed excluded but this is subject to the test of reasonableness.

We have focused on the supply of goods via a website. The law, though, affords similar implied protection for consumers shopping online where the music company is supplying a service. This time the governing legislation is the Supply of Goods and Services Act 1982. The requirement of this legislation is simple enough to grasp, though harder to test. It is that the supplier will

---

3   Sale of Goods Act 1979 Section 13(1).
4   Sale of Goods Act 1979 Section 14(2).
5   Sale of Goods Act 1979 Section 14(3.)

carry out the services with reasonable care and skill.[6] Second, where the time for the services to be carried out is not specified in the contract, but determined by a course of dealing between the parties, or left to be fixed in a manner agreed by the contract, the supplier will carry out the service within a reasonable time.[7] The same principle applies to the payment to be made for the services. Where the consideration for the services to be carried out is not specified in the contract, but determined by a course of dealing, or to be agreed by the parties, the recipient of the services will pay a reasonable charge.[8] In view of the implied requirement, it is always better for the music company to fix the price of any services provided via the website.

One should note the constant reference to consideration as opposed to money. The law refers to a valid contract having consideration as a constituent part of its ingredients. Consideration can be money or moneys worth. It might be that an online visitor can claim merchandise or the benefit of services on the website but the visitor must do something in return, not necessarily pay a sum of money. A contract can therefore be valid and satisfy the need for consideration in a number of forms.

Once again, it is apparent that the framing of the website terms must be undertaken carefully. The position alters between selling merchandise online to consumers, and selling those goods to a business purchaser. The most effective treatment of the problem is for the online music business to have a satisfactory quality management and returns policy in place as a matter of commercial good sense. The use of legal terms, particularly those that seek to limit liability, offer further control over commercial exposure which in the context of Internet sales is attractive. However, to ensure repeat Internet traffic, first-class service is always the best policy.

We now turn to the matter of data collection via the music website. The Internet of course has made possible the capture of data to a degree hitherto not possible. It is that information which in many ways makes the medium so effective as a commercial tool. The data does not just include personal information in the form of a person's name and address. Software tracking devices enable Internet vendors to streamline the supply of goods and services to the visitor based on that visitor's previous buying behaviour. Recommendations as to other related purchases can be brought to their attention and thus, greater sales achieved by this clever deployment of technology.

---

6   Supply of Goods and Services Act 1982 Section 13.
7   Supply of Goods and Services Act 1982 Section 14(1).
8   Supply of Goods and Services Act 1982 Section 14(1).

As we will see in Chapter 7 in our review of the data protection regime, there are however strict controls in the use of personally identifiable information in the EU. Those controls have huge significance to Internet trade, and the online music business must be cognizant of their legal obligations. The place to comply with those obligations is in the website terms.

SUPPLY OF MUSIC DOWNLOADS

EXAMPLE CLAUSES FOR A MUSIC DOWNLOAD SERVICE

We have examined the typical issues covered by the terms and conditions for the supply of physical music CDs and merchandise over the Internet. We will now consider the provisions one would find in the terms and conditions for the supply of a music download service.

The terms govern the basis upon which the music business will provide the download service to consumers. They will be expressed to cover the United Kingdom only if the service is offered by a UK-based music service provider. They will state that the music files will be made available to the consumer for them to download upon payment authorization. Until the consumer's payment has been authorized no contract will have been concluded. To emphasize the point that the download service is an invitation to treat and not an offer for sale (see Chapter 2), the terms will usually say that the music business may decline to supply the downloads at any point up until the contract comes into existence (that is, upon payment authorization).

The terms will make it clear that the downloads are offered for the consumer's private non-commercial use only. There will be a total bar on the consumer copying, reproducing, lending, hiring, broadcasting, conducting a public performance or any other form of distribution of the downloads. Any such unauthorized activity will constitute a copyright infringement.

In Chapter 5 we consider the Copyright and Related Rights Regulations 2003 and the prohibition on circumventing technological measures designed to protect the rights of copyright holders. In the download terms, a provision would usually be included stating that the downloads contain security technology which ensures they may only be used in accordance with the download service. If the consumer attempts to circumvent the security technology, or assists others in so doing, it will be a breach of the terms of the download service (and of course an offence under the Regulations considered in Chapter 5). The download files will be watermarked with the information concerning the consumer's purchase of the file. Any infringement of the service by the consumer will therefore be tracked by the music business, and can be disclosed to a third party. The terms will make this clear.

In Chapter 8 we consider the effect of the Distance Selling Regulations and the cancellation rights afforded to consumers under those Regulations. Given the nature of a download service, those Regulations do not apply. The terms will state that once payment has been made for the files, the consumer cannot cancel their purchase of the downloads. The only circumstance the files may be returned to the music business is if they are defective. The music business will usually provide a replacement file or a refund.

It is not uncommon for contemporary music to feature lyrics which may cause offence to some. The terms will make it clear that certain downloads include content which may be considered offensive by some people. The music business will exclude liability for such content but will normally mark the file with a statement warning of its content before it can be downloaded.

We examine in Chapter 9 the typical payment provisions for the purchase of music content, whether physical products, ringtones or download services. The terms will state how payment can be made and if there is any charge for the use of a credit card facility for example, these must be highlighted. The music business will seek to limit its total financial liability under the terms of the service to the amount paid by the consumer for the download files in aggregate.

The terms governing the download service will be subject to English law and to address the data protection requirements under the Data Protection Act 1998 the terms will contain an appropriate privacy statement.

The E-Commerce Regulations which we examine in Chapter 4 apply to the music download service and so all the necessary information demanded by those Regulations must be set out, including for example, the physical address of the music business.

CHECKLIST

- Ensure that the music website has properly drafted legal terms and conditions.

- Instruct the website developer to construct the website to enable a click-wrap confirmation of acceptance of the terms and conditions.

- Be certain that the music business can fulfil orders placed online and meet the delivery times expressed in the terms and conditions.

- Consider whether the music business needs to restrict its online activity to certain countries only.

- Ensure a governing law clause is included in the terms and conditions.

- Note the distinction between terms and conditions for providing CDs, DVDs and other physical merchandise, and those governing music download services.

CHAPTER 4

E-Commerce Regulations 2002

OPERATING MUSIC WEBSITES WITHIN THE LAW

In 2002 in response to a growing concern that consumers might become unwitting victims of virtual businesses which operate only online and who cannot be traced if they do not honour their obligations, the EU introduced a set of Regulations. These are designed to provide consumers throughout the EU with more comfort when buying goods or services over the Internet. This protection only applies to consumers who visit commercial websites but the requirements which the Regulations set down clearly dictate how any business website must operate.

In the UK the Regulations are called the Electronic Commerce (EC Directive) Regulations 2002 (SI 2002 No. 2013). They transpose the main requirements of the EU's E-Commerce Directive (2000/31/EC) into UK law.

Every record company website which offers merchandise or services must comply with the Regulations as must any website connected with the music industry where that website sells products or services. Failure to comply can lead to prosecution by the Trading Standards Department or Office of Fair Trading.

The E-Commerce Regulations (the Regulations) seek to encourage greater use of e-commerce by removing barriers across Europe and enhance consumer confidence by clarifying the rights and obligations of business and consumers.

The Regulations also seek to promote the single market in Europe by ensuring the free movement of information society services across the European Economic Area. That area of course includes the 25 member states of the EU together with Iceland, Norway and Liechtenstein. The term 'information society services' essentially means all commercial online services.

The Regulations have great relevance to the entertainment industry given that they have application to a music business if it advertises goods or services online. This includes:

- via the Internet

- on interactive television

- by mobile telephones.

Each of these routes to market lend themselves to the music industry and its predominantly youth market.

The Regulations cover a number of aspects of electronic trade including provisions for the national law that will apply to online services.

In addition they cover the information a music business must give to its online consumers. These details include discounts and offers which might feature in an online advertising campaign and how to conclude contracts on its website.

The Regulations also set out limitations on a service provider's liability for unlawful information it unwittingly carries or stores.

If a music business wishes to sell merchandise or render some service via its website it must meet its legal obligations enshrined in the Regulations. Non-compliance has consequences. For example, a fan who purchased an artist's latest CD from the website may cancel their order. They may seek a court order against the music business. They may also sue the company for breach of statutory duty if they can demonstrate that they have suffered loss because of the company's failure to comply with the Regulations.

If a music business operates a website which does not comply with the Regulations there are penalties which in addition to the financial consequence would also cause considerable damage to goodwill. Allied to the Regulations are the Stop Now Orders (EC Directive) Regulations 2001. These permit the Director Generals of Fair Trading and Trading Standards Departments in the UK to apply to the Court for a Stop Now Order if the music business's failure to comply with the Regulations 'harms the collective interest of consumers'. The Stop Now Order requires the music business to immediately cease operation of its website and take it offline. When one considers how vital the website might be to the company and perhaps the numerous merchandise and services provided via the website, it can be seen that a Stop Now Order must be avoided. The website must remain offline until the corrective work has been completed. Given the significant financial loss that could ensue from the enforced shutdown it is obviously important for music business website operators to ensure their websites comply with the Regulations in the first place.

The courts also have the power to order the publication of corrective statements with a view to eliminating the continuing effects of past infringements. Failure by a music company to comply with a Stop Now Order could result in its being held in contempt of court. The consequence of that might be a fine and/or imprisonment of its principal officers or directors.

There are a number of organizations which can enforce the Regulations. Examples include Trading Standards Departments, the Office of Fair Trading and the Independent Committee for the Supervision of Standards of Telephone Information Services (ICSTIS). It is important to appreciate that the risk of being identified as being in breach of the Regulations is high. Any consumer who might visit the music website can report the company to the appropriate body with a view to, for example, the Trading Standards Department then taking action against the music company.

The E-Commerce Regulations also impact the question of whose law will apply to cross-border trade. Clearly, the distribution of music either by dispatch of music CDs or DVDs to another country or by online means is common. The Regulations liberalize the provision of online services in two key ways. First, they require a UK-established music business to comply with UK laws even if it is providing those services in another member state. In other words, the UK-established music company will have to comply with UK law even if it is providing its services to, for example, German recipients.

The Regulations also prevent the UK from restricting the provision of information society services from another member state in the EU. In essence, there is nothing to stop for example a French music business based in Paris from providing web-based music services available in the UK and target towards the UK music-buying consumers.

However, these rules are subject to a number of qualifications and exclusions. We examine in Chapter 15 the importance of specifying which country's law will govern the online contract. The Regulations also include the freedom to choose the law which applies to an online contract and specify certain contractual obligations with regard to consumer contracts made over the Internet.

The Regulations do not, however, deal with the jurisdiction of the courts; that is, for example, which court will hear a cross-border trading dispute between a record company based in the UK and an online games company based in Spain.

NEW INFORMATION REQUIREMENTS

The Information Requirements contained in the Regulations can be divided into three categories.

INFORMATION REQUIREMENTS

The music business must provide its consumer end users with full contract details of the organization and details of any relevant trade organizations to which it belongs, for example the British Phonographic Industry (BPI). Details of any authorization scheme relevant to its online business must also be made clear. If the business is making available merchandise or services via its website it will almost certainly fall within the VAT threshold. If so, its VAT Registration number must be published on the website. There must be a clear indication of prices for the merchandise or service including any delivery or tax charges.

COMMERCIAL COMMUNICATIONS

The Regulations impose an obligation on the music company to provide its online customers with clear information concerning any electronic communications which are designed to promote (directly or indirectly) its merchandise, services or image.

Examples of such electronic communications would include emails advertising its merchandise or services. In Chapter 12 we examine the broader requirements the company must adhere to in terms of its online advertising. The E-Commerce Regulations build on those.

The music business must provide clear identification of the person on whose behalf the communication is sent. For example, the email header might read 'Unsolicited Commercial Communication sent on behalf of Lecote Records Ltd'. In addition, full details of any promotional offers advertised, for example, any discounts on merchandise, premium gifts, band or artist competitions or games must be provided. If the music business wishes to impose any qualifying conditions upon such special offers a full explanation of those conditions must be given.

ELECTRONIC CONTRACTS

As we have seen in Chapter 2 in relation to the formation of online contracts the method by which a contract must be created over the Internet is subject to a number of issues. The E-Commerce Regulations add to those more general stipulations. The essential information which a music business must provide its online consumers with is as follows.

The business must provide a description of the different technical steps to be taken to conclude a contract online. In other words, there must be clear guidance on the website as to how the contract to purchase a DVD, for example, is completed. We saw in our review of the music company's Internet legal terms and conditions how those terms must be clicked through before the online consumer can proceed to the checkout section of the website. The Regulations say that it must be clear to the buyer the point at which they will be legally bound. There must be no ambiguity. Further, the company must provide confirmation of whether the contract will be filed by the company and whether it can be accessed. A clear identification of the technical means to enable its online customers to correct any inputting errors must be shown.

It may be that the record company operates across many jurisdictions or targets certain merchandise or services to particular countries. If this is the case an indication of the languages offered in which to conclude the contract must be displayed.

Remember, all these requirements embodied in the Regulations relating to electronic contracting apply to any music business which advertises or sells merchandise or services via the Internet, mobile phone or interactive television.

So, let us consider in more detail the requirements of the E-Commerce Regulations.

The UK Government recognizes that technological constraints, for example the 160-character limit on a mobile text message, may mean that the music company may not be able to provide all the information required by the Regulations via the same means by which it transacts with its customer. The

Government believes that the information requirements outlined above will be met if the information is accessible by other means.

For example, if the online consumer purchases a music download via their mobile phone, the record company should be able to satisfy its requirements if it places the relevant information on its principal website.

Temporary interruptions to online services do arise from time to time. We saw in our review of the music business's website terms and conditions why it is important for the company to exclude liability for occasional transient disruption to its online service. The Government also appreciates that temporary interruptions to the availability of information are essential, for example for maintenance purposes, or unavoidable, for example if the computer system crashes because of a virus. Such interruptions will not place the music business in breach of its legal obligations.

The point to appreciate is that the information requirements summarized above are in addition to other legal requirements. These include those under the Consumer Protection (Contracts Concluded at a Distance) Regulations 2000 which are discussed in Chapter 8. Those Regulations, among other things require the company to provide a description of its merchandise or services, details of any guarantees offered and full details of its online customers' rights to cancel an order.

The website terms and conditions applicable to the music business's online contract must be made available in a way which allows the consumer to store and reproduce them. It is considered that this requirement will be satisfied if end users are able to save the terms and conditions onto their computer and subsequently print them out.

When the consumer places an online order with the music business it is necessary for the company to acknowledge receipt of the order without undue delay and by electronic means. It is important to remind the reader that this requirement does not apply to online transactions between two businesses, known as business-to-business transactions, if both parties agree to opt out of the Regulations. We examined in our review of online contracts generally in Chapter 2 the distinction between an offer and an invitation to treat and the dangers of sending an automatic electronic bounce-back message to enquirers. It is therefore very important when adopting the form of electronic acknowledgement required by the Regulations that the text of that acknowledgement makes it clear that the acknowledgement is not a formal acceptance of the music company's online customer enquiry.

The E-Commerce Regulations also limit the liability of ISPs who unwittingly carry or store unlawful content provided by others in certain circumstances. If a music business wishes to strike a deal with one of the ISPs for the making available of music via the ISP, the ISP will almost certainly include a confirmatory clause in the agreement excluding their liability for certain content.

REFORM OF THE E-COMMERCE REGULATIONS

At the time of publication the UK Government is seeking views on whether the protection given to ISPs under the E-Commerce Regulations should be extended to cover providers of search engines and directories, providers of keyword advertising services and content aggregators. The Government wants to assess whether the existing law is creating problems for providers of these services and if so, whether an amendment to the Regulations is necessary. One problem which could arise for example is where a search engine links to music copyright material. The link potentially helps people to copy that material – someone can infringe copyright by authorizing another to copy without the permission of the copyright owner. It is arguable that the link may itself be copyright infringement.

CHECKLIST

- Ensure that the music website contains full information about the operator including physical address and VAT number.

- If sending electronic marketing messages to promote an artist or merchandise, ensure it contains the appropriate email header. Note also to whom unsolicited emails must be sent under the Privacy and Electronic Communications Regulations discussed in Chapter 6.

- Check that the legal terms and conditions on the music website are capable of being printed off by the online customer.

- Ensure that the visitor to the website is made fully aware of the steps necessary to conclude a contract via the music website.

- If using mobile phone text messaging to alert customers about marketing offers, ensure that a suitable clear reference is included to the music website and the legal terms and conditions contained on that website.

CHAPTER 5

Protecting and Exploiting Intellectual Property Rights in Online Music

COPYRIGHT AND THE INTERNET IN GENERAL

A website operated by a music business will contain many elements, each of which will attract copyright protection: the website's text, graphics, advertisements, data and of course music. Thus, the suggestion that there is no such thing as copyright on the Internet is clearly misplaced.

Copyright is a negative right. It is a right to restrain others from exploiting work without the owner's consent.

In this country copyright is governed by the Copyright, Designs and Patents Act 1988 which came into effect in 1989. Section 1(1) of that Act states that copyright may subsist in the following types of work:

- original literary, dramatic, musical or artistic works;

- sound recordings, films, broadcasts or cable programmes;

- the typographical arrangement of published editions.

For a literary, dramatic, musical or artistic work to qualify for protection it must be original. This does not mean that for example the music needs to be novel or unique: it only has to originate from the writer, which means it must not be copied from any other work, and to embody a minimal degree of skill, judgment and labour.

Section 5A(1) states that sound recording copyright can subsist regardless of the medium on which the recording is made or the method by which the sounds are reproduced or produced.

For someone to gain the protection of the Act they must be a *qualified person*. There are three ways in which to be so qualified. They must be British citizens, domiciled here or, if a company, be incorporated in the UK. Alternatively the work must be first published in the UK. Here lies a problem for the Internet. It is not easy to be clear in which country a work is said to be first published. The third route is where the work is a broadcast or cable programme and is made or sent from the UK. Here again, problems can arise with the Internet. However, it is rare for a work in the UK not to attract copyright protection because it has not met the above tests for qualification.

The *author* is the person who creates the work, for example, the composer of the music. The author is not always the *owner* of the work. Ownership may be assigned to, for example, a music publishing company or record company by the composer.

The matter of how long a copyright work lasts is now dealt with in the Copyright and Related Rights Regulations 2003, which are considered in detail below.

CONVERGENCE OF MEDIA AND TECHNOLOGY

The rise in digital communications has changed the media landscape. Before we consider the laws which govern copyright in the digital age it is well to view that landscape fully as it affords a helpful background as to why the law is so vital. The UK appears set to become the digital media capital. Growth in digital television and broadband has been rapid and the evidence is that consumers are accessing their media content via radio, television and the Internet digitally.

The *Communications Market 2004 Report* by Ofcom, published in August 2004, serves as a useful barometer of where we are as a nation in terms of adoption of digital technology. According to the research 53 per cent of homes in the UK receive digital television. The surge in viewers using digital TV has been driven by subscription revenue, which has overtaken advertising revenue. It is interactive services which have proved to yield the highest demand. It is believed that by 2016 at least half of all programming will be accessed on-demand as technological advances make TV content more accessible.

Digital radio has also achieved dramatic growth with 2.5 per cent of UK households owning a DAB set. This is significant given the relative infancy of the format. The UK is the world leader in DAB digital radio.

In this book there is frequent reference to the convergence of media and technology and this is the issue which in many instances is causing the law difficulty. The convergence of traditional broadcasting and digital media is forcing the worlds of the television, the PC and the mobile phone together, creating significant challenges and opportunities for licensing content across these new media channels. Convergence is picked up by the report, which highlights evidence of crossover in formats. Almost 29 per cent of all adults have listened to radio using their television set. Half of all analogue radio stations can be heard through websites. The proliferation of TV delivered via the Internet, digital radio delivered via TV and several other permutations shows the huge shift that has occurred in recent years. Listening to radio via mobile phones has increased rapidly among 15–24 year olds. In 2004 one major radio group announced the launch of a 'hear it, buy it, burn it' service on its websites. Users can hear a song they like on the radio and then use the station's websites to download it to their MP3 player. A few years ago no one could have predicted that Nokia, the mobile phone manufacturer, would be the biggest suppliers of cameras. However, camera phones have proved hugely successful among consumers. Similarly, many observers find it interesting that iTunes, a technology company with no background in media content retailing, is now the market leader. The company claims that it accounts for four out of every five digital music sales in the UK. People in a very short space of time are learning to use mobile devices to watch TV, play games and listen to music. Laptops can be turned into TVs via services which stream content from cable or satellite boxes over the Internet. The mobile phone industry is starting to deliver TV channels over its wireless networks. Services which are set for launch include Visual Radio, which lets the user listen to the radio on their phones while viewing related information, such as pictures and lyrics. It is becoming clear that interactivity engages listeners and the advantages to the music company is that branding is enhanced, there is added visual appeal and they can deliver effective messaging to listeners.

There can be little doubt that the future is digital as there is a growing appetite for the delivery of all content, including entertainment, news and of course music in digital formats. Music retailer HMV claimed that before it launched its Internet music service it received around 20 CDs a week in its stores from unsigned bands and held over 400 live performances in those stores. The company proposes collecting this music and making it available, which prior to Internet distribution was not practical. In 2004 Universal Music UK, which has 26 per cent of the UK music sector and a portfolio of over 300 000 digitized tracks, launched a new service to enable the secure distribution of its music and video portfolio to mobile phones and handheld devices.

There is significant opportunity for the music industry to embrace all these platforms to increase market share but the plethora of apparatus creates legal complexities.

Combined with this convergence of media and technology has of course come the illicit distribution of music via the Internet. Until recently the only way a music company could reproduce and distribute its artists' music was to make recordings of an artist's performances, which were then mastered and distributed as physical copies such as tapes and CDs. In the very early phase of the Internet the real threat to music company revenues was the mail order sales of music CDs. As a result there was consolidation in the retail and distribution sectors. Many major record companies have withdrawn from distribution, instead entering into deals with distribution specialists. Whilst there have been some savings by music companies on warehouse and storage costs these have not been great given the strong market in the online sales of physical CDs.

However, the threat posed by Internet music piracy to the established music industry is very real. Technological changes have always created problems for music artists. From the development of music cassettes capable of recording music from 33 and 45 rpm records or off-air from the radio it has been a fact of modern commercial life. With the advent of the home computer and the Internet, together with broadband availability, the problem has been made significantly worse. Today many PCs are equipped with a CD burner as standard. Software allows users to create their own music CDs and a number of devices including MP3 players can also be used to play music that has been downloaded from the Internet. The entertainment industry claims that this file trading has significantly harmed its revenues and that the harm will only worsen as Internet technology improves.

The issue of course is a global one and not restricted to the UK music industry. There exist a variety of *peer-to-peer* Internet services which will supply music for free in contravention of copyright. Peer-to-peer websites represent the *superdistribution* of music. File-sharing networks represent the greatest library of music in history. However, it seemed that those who sourced their music in this way did not have any sense that they were causing any hardship or that digital theft was wrong. Essentially the attitude was that if it is so easy and so widespread then it cannot be illegal. In addition, this attitude was fuelled by the fact that from the early stirrings of e-commerce much of the content available from the Internet was free. The position was not sustainable and now there is a far higher proportion of online content which is paid for and expected to be so. There was also a feeling that consumers were getting their own back on an industry perceived to be charging inflated prices for CDs. So in common with other content, during the early period of music being sourced online, most of that availability was accessed for free.

However, the ability to obtain music without payment is not the only attraction of the Internet as a means of distribution. Many of those who download music do so because of the immediacy of access to music tracks rather than acquiring perhaps a CD, albeit purchased online. The Internet, though, made possible the acquisition of songs from websites set up without the permission of the copyright holder, be they artist or record company. Within a very short time these websites were attracting huge audiences because the catalogue of music they featured included current chart material both of singles and albums. There was a clear correlation between an alarming decrease in legitimate music online sales with an increase in peer-to-peer file sharing. The Internet had the clear potential to become a zone for lawlessness where the normal rules of copyright do not apply.

This threat was increased with the arrival of compression programs of which there are several types but the best known is MP3. The system developed to allow users to copy their CDs in MP3 format to be downloadable either to play at home or on MP3 players for use in mobile players or in the car.

So then began the fight back by the record industry in an effort to win the hearts and minds of consumers, combined with a use of the law to scare off would-be music file sharers.

A helpful starting point when reviewing whether merely providing the means to make illegal copies attracts legal liability is the 1984 *Sony* or 'Betamax' case. The Supreme Court of the United States had to decide whether the Betamax video machine was an illegal instrument of contributory copyright infringement. In *Sony* v *Universal City Studios* 104 US 774 (1984) the Court had to determine the legality of the Betamax machine which could both play pre-recorded films and videos legally and also could be used to record illegally. The Court held that the machine was not illegal. The UK case of *CBS Songs* v *Amstrad* (1988) RPC 567 came to a similar conclusion. The House of Lords held that there was no infringement of copyright in the marketing of a twin cassette deck which could clearly be used for infringing purposes – that of copying music cassettes without permission. It has therefore been apparent for some time that the provision of a service or equipment to facilitate copying, where that service or equipment has other legitimate uses, may not be an infringement or illegal.

The new laws considered below clearly provide the means to protect against unlawful music downloads but they do leave some anomalies. One can acquire an unwanted music CD free with a weekend newspaper yet be subject to a fine if one downloads the same music from the Internet. If someone spends a day listening to the radio and recording tracks for their MP3 player then that is to all practical purposes acceptable. However, if they download the same songs from the Internet into their iPod, that is caught by the new Regulations.

Other commentators make the point that one consequence of the Internet is that thousands of songs have suddenly become available that would not physically fit on the shelves of those who acquire them. Should record companies have the right to extract royalties from songs that would not have seen the light of day but for the long tail of the Internet?

For all the efforts of the industry there is likely to be a degree to which they will always be helpless against the practical power of the Internet. Many international recording artists have been forced to bring forward the release dates of their music albums after their songs have appeared online before reaching the shops. The fact is that as soon as something is recorded there is a real risk that it will find its way on to the Internet.

More recently the entertainment industries have turned their attention to the Internet and in particular the Internet service providers, telecommunications companies and software providers such as Verizon, Napster and Aimster.

DEVELOPMENT OF CASE LAW SURROUNDING ONLINE MUSIC

It is useful to review how the courts have approached the development of distributing music over the Internet without the copyright holders' consent. In recent years a number of software programs became available which enabled the user to download music tracks via their PC either at home or at work. The music could be obtained free as it had been uploaded as a file by someone else and through the power of the Internet as a superdistribution channel, those works could be accessed anywhere in the world. The form of these software programs has altered and the manner in which music is accessed for free without the copyright holders' consent is important in determining the precise legal basis for objection.

The largest market for music distribution and Internet use is the US and therefore it is of little surprise that the majority of the case law which has determined the issue is North American. Nonetheless those cases serve as clear guidance as to how the UK has approached the problem both in terms of policy and legal argument.

In the US the equivalent body to the UK's British Phonographic Industry (BPI) is the Recording Industry Association of America (RIAA). The RIAA, faced with the explosion of Internet file swappers downloading music from the Internet for free, decided to take direct legal action. The RIAA, on behalf of the record companies as well as some artists, sought to sue Napster. The RIAA managed to obtain the subscriber and user details of those individuals whom they considered were chronic abusers of Internet download services. In 2000 the organization sought legal action in *RIAA* v *Napster* (2000). File-sharing software was made available on a central server that enabled users to see which other users had music in MP3 compressed form that they would like to acquire. This two-way link up to share music became known as peer-to-peer. Napster drew over sixty million users a day. The US District Court held that the Napster file-swapping service was illegal. Napster had raised a variety of defences to the action by the RIAA. These included the argument rehearsed in previous eras and noted above that the service had non-infringing as well as infringing uses. In addition, they argued that its service had the effect of boosting record sales and that the plaintiffs themselves were in the business of facilitating file-swapping, citing RIAA member Sony's manufacture of MP3 players. The court rejected all these arguments and granted an interim injunction against the file-swapping service. Napster was found to have facilitated illegal copying by individual users and were ordered to pay significant damages. The company could not survive the damages award and ceased operation. The company was declared bankrupt in 2002. The suspension of the Napster service drove users to other peer-to-peer websites.

The Napster case was followed by action which represented a major victory for copyright holders in the US. In *RIAA* v *Aimster* (2002) the record industry once again sought the assistance of the law in its fight against the unauthorized uploading and downloading of music. In 2001 Aimster had applied to the US District Court to have its service declared legal. The response from the RIAA (representing copyright holders) was to institute legal proceedings against Aimster alleging contributory and vicarious copyright infringements. The court accepted the RIAA arguments and determined that Aimster had clear knowledge of infringements taking place on its service. Further, Aimster had materially contributed to these infringements. In addition, Aimster could supervise the infringements if it so wanted and Aimster had benefited financially from these infringements. It was stated that Aimster was a service whose very *raison d'être* appeared to be the facilitation of and contribution to copyright infringement on a massive scale. Aimster was ordered to prevent users from uploading and downloading copyright works or cease operations if it could not do so and to employ technical measures to prevent copyright infringement.

The next case resulted in the RIAA suffering a setback: in *MGM Studios and Others* v *Grokster and StreamCast Networks* (2003) the legal tide changed. In 2001 MGM had launched legal actions against KaZaA, Grokster and StreamCast Networks for contributory and vicarious copyright infringement. Given the need for urgent determination on the question, both sides to the dispute sought an expedited ruling on liability. The court decided in favour of StreamCast Networks and Grokster. The court was able to distinguish its decision from earlier cases on the following basis:

- First, the software had non-infringing uses.

- Second, the defendants had no actual knowledge of specific infringements and could not supervise infringements. This latter point was important because, unlike the Napster system, the Grokster facility had no centralized system. File sharers on the Internet could access each other's files without recourse to a list operated by the service provider.

Alongside the legal cases being brought with some rapidity against those organizations which operated music download facilities without the consent of the copyright holders, the RIAA went about taking legal action against serial users of such services. These of course included individuals in their homes who were taking advantage of the ability to obtain music for free via the Internet. The RIAA in this tactic were seeking to make examples of those people and to send a message out to other individuals tempted to do the same thing. This approach brought to the public attention the case of Brianna Lahara who (then aged twelve) had a love of television theme music, the successful artist Christina Aguilera and the nursery song 'If You're Happy And You Know It'. Her mother agreed to pay $2000 in compensation. The RIAA issued a statement announcing the settlement and quoting the little girl as saying 'I am sorry for what I have done. I love music and don't want to hurt the artists I love.'

This tactic of making examples of individuals who download music illegally was to be followed in the UK two years later. This approach was considered by some to be a high-risk public relations strategy. Many questioned the wisdom of multi-million-pound companies suing individuals of modest means. However, the strategy of a sustained public relations campaign aimed at dissuading individuals from downloading music illegally and legal proceedings appears to have been highly effective.

In this country the courts have also been asked to decide on legality of facilitating copyright infringement. In *Sony Music Entertainment (UK) Ltd* v *EasyInternetcafé Ltd* (2003) the High Court held that EasyInternetcafés were guilty of copyright infringement by allowing customers to download music without permission and to burn CD copies of these at EasyInternet's chain of cafés.

In June 2005 the Supreme Court of the United States tried to balance the competing demands of copyright owners and technology developers in a ruling which serves as the best guide to how the US courts approach the issue. In *MGM* v *Grokster* (2005) the court held that the distributors of peer-to-peer software could be liable for infringements committed with their software. The court reached the conclusion by the use of the concept of active inducement from the US Patent Act. At the same time the court affirmed that the distributor of a product used to infringe will not incur liability by virtue of the act of distribution so long as the product is capable of a substantial non-infringing use. On the face of it the latest chapter in the Grokster saga appears to be a music industry victory. The Supreme Court reversed the United States Federal Court of Appeals Ninth Circuit decision, which had found that Grokster had no case to answer with regard to the use of its file-sharing software to transfer illegally copied files.

The plaintiffs had argued what is known as *active inducement*. Active inducement concentrates on the defendant's conduct rather than their technology. The court found that one who distributes a device with the object of promoting its use to infringe copyright, as shown by clear expression or other affirmative steps taken to foster infringement, is liable for the resulting acts of infringement by third parties.

It is considered that the decision has powered the digital future of legitimate US online businesses including file-sharing networks by making those who promote theft accountable. The concern on the part of technology innovators is that the case has created a new era of uncertainty for software innovation.

It is clear that a distributor's mere knowledge of infringing potential or actual infringement would not be enough to subject the distributor to liability.

It is possible in light of these various cases to assess some of the tests that courts might consider when reviewing software technology which has both infringing and non-infringing uses:

- Are there substantial non-infringing uses and can the defendant prove this? This was the issue in the *Sony Betamax, MGM* v *Grokster*, and *RIAA* v *Aimster* cases.

- Does the software provider have clear knowledge of infringing uses? Wilful blindness is no defence as was the decision in the *RIAA* v *Aimster*, *Grokster* and *Napster* cases.

- Is the provider able to supervise infringement if it so wanted? This issue was considered in the *EasyInternetcafé* case.

- Has the software provider materially contributed to infringements? For example, does it provide any assistance to those individuals who infringe?

- Does the software provider financially benefit from infringing uses even where the provider is not infringing itself?

There are interesting commercial dynamics behind the recent cases on the question of Internet music downloads. These surround the ownership consolidation in the music and entertainment industries. For example, AOL Time Warner is a company with businesses on both sides of the divide. It owns AOL and two major cable companies together with a major record label, film and television interests. Sony owns a major record label in Sony Music, but also is a major producer of music equipment including recording equipment and MP3 players.

Then there is the issue as to why the record industry appeared not to plan for the advent of the Internet. Some industry commentators state that the major record labels missed the boat when it came to the World Wide Web. Apple still maintains a lead with legitimate downloads of music through its iTunes service. This is in contrast to the film industry's comprehensive commercial reaction to the threat of the VHS machine. The record industry failed to implement a business plan to deal with both the threat and opportunities presented by the Internet.

At the time of writing the evidence is that fear of prosecution is deterring people from downloading music illegally. The uptake of legal download services has increased by around 75 per cent in the year 2004 to 2005. Many people who previously downloaded music from unauthorized websites claim they would download less often in the future. The platform for the UK record industry to fight back using the law is the Copyright and Related Rights Regulations 2003 considered below. The Regulations enable the protection of legal interests and the policing and enforcement of rights in music copyright across Europe. It is this framework which has assisted the British Phonographic Industry in its efforts to combat piracy in high-profile and effective legal actions. In essence the UK music industry has conducted a well-constructed media campaign supported by legal action to change the mindset of music consumers.

It has been an impressive effort. For the past few years the music industry has been predicting the death of the singles market because of illegal downloading. However, figures produced in 2005 by the British Phonographic Industry (BPI) show that single sales are increasing. In fact the figures do not offer the complete picture as they often still refer to sales of what are known as 'physical' singles. If legal downloads are included, sales of singles have soared. Far from killing the industry, downloads have given it a new lease of life. In the year 2004–5 the number of tracks sold over the Internet reached ten million. The combination of old and new has contrived to breathe new life into the pop single, sales of which had been dwindling for a decade. Sales of digital downloads in the UK increased 744 per cent in the second quarter of 2004. According to the BPI, 5 562 638 digital downloads had been sold in the second quarter of 2005, which is almost twice the level of 2004.

The effort made by the UK record industry has been matched on an international level in a coordinated global assault on Internet piracy. In 2005 the International Federation of the Phonographic Industry (IFPI) filed a new wave of criminal and civil legal actions against significant uploaders who place hundreds of copyrighted songs on the Internet file-sharing networks without the permission of the copyright owners. The action targeted 963 individuals in 11 countries including Austria, Denmark, France, Italy, Germany, the Netherlands, Finland, Ireland, Iceland, Japan and the United Kingdom. The IFPI claimed its approach had worked, citing Germany as an example where the number of files downloaded fell sharply in 2004, down 35 per cent to 382 million files compared to 602 million the previous year.

COPYRIGHT AND RELATED RIGHTS REGULATIONS 2003

BACKGROUND

How then has the law had to adapt to meet this new era? As we have noted, in English law copyright is governed by the Copyright, Designs and Patents Act 1988. This legislation brought together under one statute a good deal of previous law in the sphere of copyright, but since its introduction the world of media technology has wholly changed. It was clear that new provisions would have to be drafted to properly transpose the fundamental principles contained in the 1988 Act to address the digital age. The result of a lengthy and detailed consultation process is the Copyright and Related Rights Regulations 2003, which came into effect in England and Wales on 31 October 2003.

In essence the new Regulations attempt to clarify the rights of those who own copyright in literary, dramatic, musical or artistic work, or in a sound recording or broadcast when the media by which those works can be distributed, are multifarious. The Regulations give the songwriter or other rightholder (for example the music publisher):

- the exclusive right to do or authorize reproduction, that is the copying of their music;

- the right to distribute copies to the public;

- the right to communicate their music to the public, for example by performing, showing or playing the music in public;

- the right to broadcast the music, including making it available in a cable programme service, or making an adaptation of the music.

Infringement occurs when any of the above acts are carried out or authorized by a party without the consent or licence of the copyright owner or rightholder.

PROVISIONS RELATING TO BROADCASTS

The Regulations amend the definition of a broadcast and section 4 states that:

> 'broadcast' means an electronic transmission of visual images, sounds or other information which

(a) is transmitted for simultaneous reception by members of the public and is capable of being lawfully received by them, or

(b) is transmitted at a time determined solely by the person making the transmission for presentation to members of the public.

Broadcasting means wired or wireless. It is important to note that this definition does not include use of the Internet per se unless the transmission via the Internet accompanies another transmission by, for example, television. The section says:

Excepted from the definition of 'broadcast' is any Internet transmission unless it is

(a) a transmission taking place simultaneously on the Internet and by other means,

(b) a concurrent transmission of a live event, or

(c) a transmission of recorded moving images or sounds forming part of a programme service offered by the person responsible for making the transmission, being a service in which programmes are transmitted at scheduled times determined by that person.

So, one can see that a music concert for example which is transmitted live on TV and which is simulcast via the Internet would be included in the definition of broadcast as far as the Internet characterization of the programme is concerned.

The Regulations go on to clarify which acts are restricted by copyright in section 6 headed:

Infringement by communication to the public

(1) The communication to the public of the work is an act restricted by the copyright in:

(a) a literary, dramatic, musical or artistic work,

(b) a sound recording or film, or

(c) a broadcast.

(2) References...to communication to the public are to communication to the public by electronic transmission, and in relation to a work include:

> *(a) the broadcasting of the work,*
>
> *(b) the making available to the public of the work by electronic transmission in such a way that members of the public may access it from a place and at a time individually chosen by them.*

It appears from this section that a communication to the public is restricted whether it be by broadcast, for example TV and radio, or by electronic transmission where the public can access it where and when they like, such as the Internet or by the use of 'on-demand' services.

THE MAKING AVAILABLE RIGHT

One significant revision of the 1988 Act is the introduction of the Making Available Right for performers. Section 182CA states that consent is required for making available to the public.

> *A performer's rights are infringed by a person who, without his consent, makes available to the public a recording of the whole or any substantial part of a qualifying performance by electronic transmission in such a way that members of the public may access the recording from a place and at a time individually chosen by them.*

The right of a performer under this section to authorize or prohibit the making available to the public of a recording is referred to as the 'making available right'.

As with all copyright rules that came before the new Regulations, there are certain actions which by their nature do not constitute a significant breach of copyright and are as such permissible under the law.

Making temporary copies

Section 8 provides that:

> *The copyright…in a…musical work…is not infringed by the making of a temporary copy which is transient or incidental, which is an integral and essential part of a technological process and the sole purpose of which is to enable*
>
> *(a) a transmission of the work in a network between third parties by an intermediary; or*

(b) a lawful use of the work;

and which has no independent economic significance.

Research and private study

The Regulations also alter the definition of so called 'Fair Dealing' in copyright work. The new provision is clear enough from the following reproduction of its phrasing. Section 9 now states that:

> *Fair dealing with a...musical...work for the purpose of research for a non-commercial purpose does not infringe any copyright in the work provided that it is accompanied by a sufficient acknowledgement.*

The section goes on to say that no acknowledgment of the kind detailed above is required where this would be impossible for reasons of practicality or otherwise.

> *Further, fair dealing with a...musical...work for the purposes of private study does not infringe any copyright in the work.*

A new element to the extent of fair dealing is the clear direction in relation to computer programs. Such programs might of course be related to the online distribution of music. The new paragraph says:

> *It is not fair dealing to observe, study or test the functioning of a computer program in order to determine the ideas and principles which underlie any element of the program.*

Criticism, review and news reporting

There are also changes to the position on fair dealing in the context of criticism, review and news reporting of for example a music single or album. Section 10 says that:

> *Fair dealing with a performance or recording for the purpose of criticism or review, of that or another performance or recording, or of a work, does not infringe any of the rights...provided that the performance or recording has been made available to the public.*

Music promotion of course usually features film promotion, perhaps in the form of a video to accompany a single. In relation to the exceptions to copyright infringement, the Regulations make clear that certain things can be done with copyright musical works for the purposes of instruction or examination. The new law says that:

> *Copyright in a sound recording, film or broadcast is not infringed by its being copied by making a film or film soundtrack in the course of instruction, or of preparation for instruction, in the making of films or film soundtracks, provided the copying*
>
> *(a) is done by a person giving or receiving instruction, and*
>
> *(b) is accompanied by a sufficient acknowledgement*
>
> *and provided the instruction is for a non commercial purpose.*

There are other circumstances where certain copying is permitted but these do not require elaboration in this book. They include provisions relating to recordings by educational establishments of broadcasts, provisions relating to copying by librarians, and the observing, studying and testing of computer programs. The latter covers the situation where the study or testing of the functionality of the program is done in order to determine the ideas and principles which underlie any element of the program. If this is done while for example running the program, which one is entitled to do, then the copying is permitted.

Provisions relating to recording for the purposes of time shifting

Where a copy which would otherwise be an infringing copy is made but which is subsequently dealt with:

> *(a) it shall be treated as an infringing copy for the purposes of that dealing; and*
>
> *(b) if that dealing infringes copyright, it shall be treated as an infringing copy for all subsequent purposes.*
>
> *'Dealt with' means sold or let for hire, offered or exposed for sale or hire or communicated to the public.*

It is important to distinguish pure domestic time shifting and the Regulations state:

> *(1) The making in domestic premises for private and domestic use of a recording of a broadcast solely for the purpose of enabling it to be viewed*

or listened to at a more convenient time does not infringe any right...in relation to a performance or recording included in the broadcast.

However, the Regulations make clear:

(3) Where a recording which would otherwise be an illicit recording is made in accordance with this paragraph but is subsequently dealt with

(a) it shall be treated as an illicit recording for the purposes of that dealing; and

(b) if that dealing infringes any right...it shall be treated as an illicit recording for all subsequent purposes.

CIRCUMVENTING TECHNICAL MEASURES

It is new technologies which have created the problem of Internet piracy. It is new technologies which in many ways are the best form of resistance. The obvious answer is for record companies to install technology in their goods which would monitor when and where they were used. This would prevent music being listened to unless the copyright was identified as legitimate. Huge resources have been put into anti-piracy devices including watermarking and other methods to track the copying of music to control it and ensure proper payment. Other systems seek to create permanent and temporary passwords on computer files which permit only one copy of a file to be made and played on a legitimate player. Making one copy destroys one of the passwords and if an attempt is made to copy once more, the copy will not play because the player can only find one of the required two passwords. There are many such systems at present but they probably only make it more difficult for music pirates rather than solve the problem fully. A useful example is the difficulties presented by installing copyright protection in CDs. These contain deliberate errors which make it harder to copy the music. However, these errors mean that many legitimate CDs cannot be used in the CD drives of some computers.

Nonetheless the role of digital rights management in acquiring and delivering content for the mobile market for example is vital.

Although therefore it is very difficult to develop technology to prevent infringement, the EU and the UK by virtue of the Copyright and Related Rights Regulations 2003 insist on strict legal protections for technology-driven devices. In essence the requirement, common throughout the EU, is that member states provide adequate legal protection against the circumvention of any effective technological measures, which the person concerned carries out in the knowledge, or with reasonable grounds to know, that he or she is pursuing that objective.

Definition of technological measures

Before considering how attempts to get around technical processes designed to stop copyright infringement are unlawful, it is worth setting out how the Regulations define 'technological measures'. Section 296ZF says:

> *Technological measures are any technology, device or component which is designed, in the normal course of its operation, to protect a copyright work other than a computer program. They are 'effective' if the use of the work is controlled by the copyright owner through*
>
> *(a) an access control or protection process such as encryption, scrambling or other transformation of the work or*
>
> *(b) a copy control mechanism*
>
> *which achieves the intended protection.*
>
> *When reference is made to protecting musical works this is defined to mean the prevention or restriction of acts that are not authorized by the copyright owner and are restricted by copyright; and*
>
> *The use of the musical work does not extend to any use of the work that is outside the scope of the acts restricted by copyright.*

Circumvention of technological measures

Technical developments allow music copyright holders to make use of technological measures designed to prevent or restrict acts not authorized by them. The threat of course is that illegal activities might be carried out in order to enable or facilitate the circumvention of technical protection provided by these measures. Section 296ZA of the Regulations applies where:

> *(a) effective technological measures have been applied to a copyright work other than a computer program; and*
>
> *(b) a person (B) does anything which circumvents those measures knowing, or with reasonable grounds to know, that he is pursuing that objective.*
>
> *The following people have legal rights against B:*

(a) a person –

    (i) issuing to the public copies of, or

    (ii) communicating to the public,

the work to which effective technological measures have been applied; and

(b) the copyright owner or his exclusive licensee, if he is not the person specified in paragraph (a).

Devices and services designed to circumvent technological measures

Under Section 296ZB 'Devices and services designed to circumvent technological measures':

(1) A person commits an offence if he –

(a) manufactures for sale or hire, or

(b) imports otherwise than for his private and domestic use, or

(c) in the course of a business –

    (i) sells or lets for hire, or

    (ii) offers or exposes for sale or hire, or

    (iii) advertises for sale or hire, or

    (iv) possesses, or

    (v) distributes, or

(d) distributes otherwise than in the course of a business to such an extent as to affect prejudicially the copyright owner,

any device, product or component which is primarily designed, produced, or adapted for the purpose of enabling or facilitating the circumvention of effective technological measures.

(2) A person commits an offence if he provides, promotes, advertises or markets –

(a) in the course of a business, or

(b) otherwise than in the course of a business to such an extent as to affect prejudicially the copyright owner,

a service the purpose of which is to enable or facilitate the circumvention of effective technological measures.

Under Section (4) a person guilty of an offence under subsections (1) or (2) above is liable –

(a) on summary conviction, to imprisonment for a term not exceeding three months, or to a fine not exceeding the statutory minimum, or both;

(b) on conviction on indictment to a fine or imprisonment for a term not exceeding two years, or both.

(5) It is a defence to any prosecution for an offence under this section for the defendant to prove that he did not know, and had no reasonable grounds for believing, that –

(a) the device, product or component; or

(b) the service,

enabled or facilitated the circumvention of effective technological measures.

Who can sue those who use devices and services designed to circumvent technological measures?

The question arises as to who actually has the right to take legal action against someone who attempts to get around the copyright technical safeguards applied to a music product. Section 296ZD of the Regulations provides the answer:

If effective technological measures have been applied to a music copyright work and someone manufactures, imports, distributes, sells or advertises or simply has in his possession a device or provides services which are promoted, advertised or marketed for the purpose of the circumvention, or have only a limited commercially significant purpose other than to circumvent, or are primarily designed to enable circumvention, then the following people will have legal rights against that person:

(a) a person issuing to the public copies of or communicating to the public the musical work to which effective technological measures have been applied;

(b) the actual copyright owner or his exclusive licensee;

(c) the owner or exclusive licensee of any intellectual property right in the effective technological measures applied to the musical work.

Each of these people can take legal action against the infringer demanding delivery up or seizure of the products in question.

Electronic rights management information

The Regulations also provide legal protection in the sphere of electronic rights management. Rights management information is defined as:

...any information provided by the copyright owner or the holder of any right under copyright which identifies the work, the author, the copyright owner or the holder of any intellectual property rights, or information about the terms and conditions of use of the work, and any numbers or codes that represent such information.

Section 296ZG says:

It is unlawful where a person knowingly and without authority, removes or alters electronic rights management information associated with a copy of a copyright work. It is also unlawful if a person knows he is inducing, enabling, facilitating or concealing an infringement of copyright.

In addition, section 296ZG(2) covers someone who:

...knowingly and without authority, distributes, imports for distribution or communicates to the public, copies of a copyright work from which electronic rights management information has been removed or altered if that person knows or has reason to believe, that by so doing he is inducing, enabling, facilitating or concealing an infringement of copyright.

Criminal offences

The Regulations introduce new criminal offences in circumstances where there has been infringement as follows:

*A person who infringes copyright in a work by **communicating the work to the public***

a) in the course of a business, or

b) otherwise than in the course of a business to such an extent as to affect prejudicially the owner of the copyright, commits an offence if he knows or has reason to believe that, by doing so, he is infringing copyright in that work.

The Regulations state that a person guilty of an offence above is liable:

(a) on summary conviction to imprisonment for a term not exceeding three months or a fine not exceeding the statutory maximum, or both;

(b) on conviction on indictment to a fine or imprisonment for a term not exceeding two years, or both.

*A person who infringes a performer's **making available right***

(a) in the course of a business, or

(b) otherwise than in the course of a business to such an extent as to affect prejudicially the owner of the making available right,

commits an offence if he knows or has reason to believe that, by doing so, he is infringing the making available right in the recording.

A person guilty of an offence above is liable:

(a) on summary conviction to imprisonment for a term not exceeding three months or a fine not exceeding the statutory maximum, or both;

(b) on conviction on indictment to a fine or imprisonment for a term not exceeding two years, or both.

The Regulations also seek to enforce legal remedies against service providers in the context of copyright infringement.

The High Court has power to grant an injunction against a service provider, where the service provider has actual knowledge of another person using their service to infringe copyright.

The court clearly will have to determine whether a service provider has actual knowledge and it will take into account all matters which appear to it in the particular circumstances to be relevant. Amongst other things, the court shall have regard to:

(a) whether a service provider has received a notice which includes the full name and address of the sender of the notice and details of the infringement in question. It is important to note that the definition of

service provider in the context of the Copyright and Related Rights Regulations have the same meaning given to it by regulation 2 of the Electronic Commerce (EC Directive) Regulations 2002 [considered in Chapter 4].

The High Court also has power to grant an injunction against a service provider, where that service provider has actual knowledge of another person using their service to infringe a performer's property right. Once again, in determining whether a service provider has actual knowledge the court will apply the same test detailed above.

The Regulations provide certain rights to those who hold merely a non-exclusive license in relation to copyrighted works:

A non-exclusive licensee may bring an action for infringement of copyright if

(a) the infringing act was directly connected to a prior licensed act of the licensee, and the licence itself

(i) is in writing and is signed by or on behalf of the copyright owner, and

(ii) expressly grants the non-exclusive licensee a right of action under the section in the Regulations.

The non-exclusive licensee has the same rights and remedies as the actual copyright owner would have had if it was he who had brought the legal action. The copyright owner still of course has his own rights if he chooses to use them.

Duration of copyright in sound recordings

The Regulations amend the Copyright, Designs and Patents Act 1988 on the matter of how long copyright lasts in a work. Section 29 of the Regulations state that copyright expires:

(i) at the end of the period of 50 years from the end of the calendar year in which the recording is made, or

(ii) if during that period the recording is published, 50 years from the end of the calendar year in which it is first published, or

(iii) if during that period the recording is not published but is made available to the public by being played in public or communicated to the public, 50 years from the end of the calendar year in which it is first so made available.

But in determining whether a sound recording has been published, played in public or communicated to the public, no account shall be taken of any unauthorized act.

CREATIVE COMMONS

One interesting recent development is the availability of what is known as Creative Commons. Creative Commons began in the US in 2001 with the aim of establishing a fair middle way between the extremes of copyright control, and the unsolicited exploitation of intellectual property. The creator-led scheme encourages musicians, writers and artists to give up some of their rights, for example the right to distribute work or to control derivative works, to the 'commons' of the Internet. This is achieved via a system of off-the-peg licences that are machine-readable. Its primary tool is the use of a range of copyright licences which are freely available for public use. The licences allow creators to fine-tune control over their work to enable as wide a distribution as possible. In essence the copyright holder is able to set out terms of use when they create their work. They might for example state that they are content for others to use their work for any reason as long as it is not for commercial purposes. Alternatively they may permit use of commercial purposes. In this way, ideas can be protected, but the author is able to encourage some other uses of their work. It is in effect a label saying 'Some rights reserved' as opposed to the usual copyright protection of 'All rights reserved'. The artist keeps their copyright but allows people to copy and distribute their work provided they as writers are given credit. The idea is to give the public access to for example archive footage from the different archives so they can use it to create new things, such as making their own music video.

The Creative Commons concept has just been introduced in the UK following careful work by a legal team at Oxford University's 'Programme in Comparative Media Law and Policy'. Channel 4 in the UK is using the Creative Commons licences scheme for a music video service which it calls PIXnMIX. The concept behind Creative Commons is to allow for content to be introduced into the online environment so that it can be shared fully but also protected.

In the UK there are two different licences: one for England and Wales, and one for Scotland to reflect the differing legal jurisdictions.

Creative Commons is at an early stage of life but it has already had some impact on the music industry with some artists being persuaded to release their content under a creative commons licence.

There are some in the music industry who express concern over creative commons fearing that it undermines traditional copyright protection. They believe that songwriters may unwittingly give away their rights irrevocably. In addition it could result in musicians who sign Creative Commons licences being discounted by a music business hostile to the concept. At the time of completion of this book it is not possible to assess the likely impact creative commons will have on music distribution in the digital era.

CREATIVE COMMONS SPECIMEN LICENCE

CREATIVE COMMONS

LEGAL CODE

Attribution – NoDerivs 2.0 England and Wales

> CREATIVE COMMONS CORPORATION IS NOT A LAW FIRM AND DOES NOT PROVIDE LEGAL SERVICES. DISTRIBUTION OF THIS LICENCE DOES NOT CREATE AN ATTORNEY-CLIENT RELATIONSHIP. CREATIVE COMMONS PROVIDES THIS INFORMATION ON AN 'AS-IS' BASIS. CREATIVE COMMONS MAKES NO WARRANTIES REGARDING THE INFORMATION PROVIDED, AND DISCLAIMS LIABILITY FOR DAMAGES RESULTING FROM ITS USE.

Licence

THE WORK (AS DEFINED BELOW) IS PROVIDED UNDER THE TERMS OF THIS CREATIVE COMMONS PUBLIC LICENCE ('CCPL' OR 'LICENCE'). THE WORK IS PROTECTED BY COPYRIGHT AND/ OR OTHER APPLICABLE LAW. ANY USE OF THE WORK OTHER THAN AS AUTHORIZED UNDER THIS LICENCE OR COPYRIGHT

LAW IS PROHIBITED. BY EXERCISING ANY RIGHTS TO THE WORK PROVIDED HERE, YOU ACCEPT AND AGREE TO BE BOUND BY THE TERMS OF THIS LICENCE. THE LICENSOR GRANTS YOU THE RIGHTS CONTAINED HERE IN CONSIDERATION OF YOUR ACCEPTANCE OF SUCH TERMS AND CONDITIONS.

This Creative Commons England and Wales Public Licence enables You (all capitalized terms defined below) to view, edit, modify, translate and distribute Works worldwide, under the terms of this licence, provided that You credit the Original Author.

'The Licensor' (one or more legally recognized persons or entities offering the Work under the terms and conditions of this Licence)

and

'You'

agree as follows:

1. Definitions

a. **'Attribution'** means acknowledging all the parties who have contributed to and have rights in the Work or Collective Work under this Licence.

b. **'Collective Work'** means the Work in its entirety in unmodified form along with a number of other separate and independent works, assembled into collective whole.

c. **'Derivative Work'** means any work created by the editing, modification, adaptation or translation of the Work in any media (however a work that constitutes a Collective Work will not be considered a Derivative Work for the purposes of this Licence). For the avoidance of doubt, where the Work is a musical composition or sound recording, the synchronization of the Work in timed-relation with a moving image ('synching') will be considered a Derivative Work for the purpose of this Licence.

d. **'Licence'** means this Creative Commons England and Wales Public Licence agreement.

e. **'Original Author'** means the individual (or entity) who created the Work.

f. **'Work'** means the work protected by copyright which is offered under the terms of this Licence.

g. For the purpose of this Licence, when not inconsistent with the contracts, words in the singular number include the plural number.

2. Licence Terms

2.1 The Licensor hereby grants to You a worldwide, royalty-free, non-exclusive, Licence for use and for the duration of copyright in the Work.

You may:

- copy the Work;

- incorporate the Work into one or more Collective Work; and

- publish, distribute, archive, perform or otherwise disseminate the Work or the Work as incorporated in any Collective Work to the public in any material form in any media whether now known or hereafter created.

HOWEVER,

You must not:

- impose any terms on the use to be made of the Work or the Work as incorporated in a Collective Work that alter or restrict the terms of this Licence or any rights granted under it or has the effect or intent of restricting the ability to exercise those rights;

- impose any digital rights management technology on the Work or the Work as incorporated in a Collective Work that alters or restricts the terms of this Licence or any rights granted under it or has the effect or intent of restricting the ability to exercise those rights;

- make any Derivative Works;

- sublicense the Work;

- subject the Work to any derogatory treatment as defined in the Copyright, Designs and Patents Act 1988.

FINALLY,

You must:

- make reference to this Licence (by Uniform Resource Identifier (URI), spoken word or as appropriate to the media used) on all copies of the Work and Collective Works published, distributed, performed or otherwise disseminated or made available to the public by You;

- recognize the Licensor's/Original Author's rights of attribution in any Work and Collective Work that You publish, distribute, perform or otherwise disseminate to the public and ensure that You credit the Licensor/Original Author as appropriate to the media used; and

- to the extent reasonably practicable, keep intact all notices that refer to this Licence, in particular the URI, if any, that the Licensor specifies to be associated with the Work, unless such URI does not refer to the copyright notice or licensing information for the Work.

Additional Provisions for third parties making use of the Work

2.2 Further licence from the Licensor

Each time You publish, distribute, perform or otherwise disseminate

- the Work; or

- the Work as incorporated in a Collective Work

the Licensor agrees to offer to the relevant third party making use of the Work (in any of the alternatives set out above) a licence to use the Work on the same terms and conditions as granted to You hereunder.

2.3 This Licence does not affect any rights that the User may have under any applicable law, including fair use, fair dealing or any other legally recognized limitation or exception to copyright infringement.

2.4 All rights not expressly granted by the Licensor are hereby reserved, including but not limited to, the exclusive right to collect, whether individually or via a licensing body, such as a collecting society, royalties for any use of the Work.

3. Warranties and Disclaimer

Except as required by law, the Work is licensed by the Licensor on an 'as-is' and 'as-available' basis and without any warranty of any kind, either express or implied.

4. Limit of Liability

Subject to any liability which may not be excluded or limited by law the Licensor shall not be liable and hereby expressly excludes all liability for loss or damage howsoever and whenever caused to You.

5. Termination

The rights granted to You under this Licence shall terminate automatically upon any breach by You of the terms of this Licence. Individuals or entities who have received Collective Works from You under this Licence, however will not have their Licences terminated provided such individuals or entities remain in full compliance with those Licences.

6. General

6.1 The validity or enforcement of the remaining terms of this agreement is not affected by the holding of any provision of it to be invalid or unenforceable.

6.2 This Licence constitutes the entire Licence Agreement between the parties with respect to the Work licensed here. There are no understandings, agreements or representations with respect to the Work not specified here. The Licensor shall not be bound by any additional provisions that may appear in any communication in any form.

6.3 A person who is not a party to this Licence shall have no rights under the Contracts (Rights of Third Parties) Act 1999 to enforce any of its terms.

6.4 This Licence shall be governed by the law of England and Wales and the parties irrevocably submit to the exclusive jurisdiction of the Courts of England and Wales.

7. On the role of Creative Commons

7.1 Neither the Licensor nor the User may use the Creative Commons logo except to indicate that the Work is licensed under a Creative Commons Licence. Any permitted use has to be in compliance with the Creative Commons trademark usage guidelines at the time of use of the Creative Commons trademark. These guidelines may be found on the Creative Commons website or be otherwise available upon request from time to time.

7.2 Creative Commons Corporation does not profit from its role in providing this Licence and will not investigate the claims of any Licensor or user of the Licence.

7.3 One of the conditions that Creative Commons Corporation requires of the Licensor and You is an acknowledgment of its limited roles and agreement by all who use the Licence that the Corporation is not responsible to anyone for the statements and actions of You or the Licensor or anyone else attempting to use this Licence.

7.4 Creative Commons Corporation is not a party to this Licence, and makes no warranty whatsoever in connection to the Work or in connection to this Licence, and in all events is not liable for any loss or damage resulting from the Licensor's or Your reliance on this Licence or on its enforceability.

7.5 USE OF THIS LICENCE MEANS THAT YOU AND THE LICENSOR EACH ACCEPTS THESE CONDITIONS IN SECTION 7.1, 7.2, 7.3 AND 7.4 AND EACH ACKNOWEDGES CREATIVE COMMONS CORPORATION'S VERY LIMITED ROLE AS A FACILITATOR OF THE LICENCE FROM THE LICENSOR TO YOU.

Creative Commons is not a party to this Licence, and makes no warranty whatsoever in connection with the Work. Creative Commons will not be liable to You or any party on any legal theory for any damages whatsoever, including without limitation any general, special, incidental or consequential damages arising in connection to this Licence.

Notwithstanding the foregoing two (2) sentences, if Creative Commons has expressly identified itself as the Licensor hereunder, it shall have all rights and obligations of Licensor.

Except for the limited purpose of indicating to the public that the Work is licensed under the CCPL, neither party will use the trademark 'Creative Commons' or any related trademark or logo of Creative Commons without the prior written consent of Creative Commons. Any permitted use will be in compliance with Creative Commons' then current trademark usage guidelines, as may be published on its website or otherwise made available upon request from time to time.

Creative Commons may be contacted at http://creativecommons.org/.

PODCASTING

A very recent development in the sphere of Internet communications is the broadcasting of audio files online, dominated by the use of MP3 files. This practice has been dubbed *podcasting*, which is a description that can be misleading given that one does not require an Apple iPod in order to participate. The attraction of making audio files available on a website is that visitors can download them and listen at their own convenience on their PCs or portable players. With the increased availability of broadband permitting faster upload and download speeds, podcasting has come into its own.

Podcast audio files can be used for example to provide an audio feed with news or updates about a recording artist in much the same way that websites already provide articles and short news items. In some cases podcasting has seen the use of portable players to generate music shows which can be accessed as stated at any time by the recipient. Such broadcasts fall outside the scope of any traditional broadcast regulation.

The process of podcasting is simple requiring only a good microphone and audio software for recording in the MP3 format. One needs to create a feed with a link to the audio file and upload the file to a website. Making the feed involves using a very short piece of code describing what the audio file is and what it is about. Listeners can either save the files when they visit the website or subscribe to the feed and download them automatically.

On a positive note the emergence of podcasting might see the development of a genuinely innovative form of mobile broadcast providing an unmatched freedom and interactivity to a new generation of listeners.

EXAMPLE MODELS FOR LEGITIMATE MUSIC DOWNLOADS

A number of companies offering legitimate music download services have emerged in recent times and appear to be performing very well. Indeed such is their market that the Official UK Chart decided in 2004 to include online music downloads in the chart rankings for singles. On the face of it each of these companies offer identical services. However, there are a variety of business models which also impact on the cost of the downloads.

The new Napster for example is primarily a subscription service which seeks to build a community around its users. For a monthly fee, unlimited downloads can be accessed onto the hard drives of up to three PCs. There is a further small fee per track to copy the track to a CD or transfer to a portable device. The songs are downloaded in the encrypted Windows Media Audio format, which can be transferred to sixty different portable players but not including Apple's iPod. Napster also operates ten interactive radio stations and its community services include a personalized radio station that is automatically created by selecting three songs. The subscribers can browse each other's playlists and share songs via email.

Another model is Apple's iTunes. At the time of writing it has a library of around 700 000 songs. There is a small fee per track and the tracks can be shared by up to five computers on a network, burnt an unlimited number of times to CD and copied to an unlimited number of iPods. The songs are in Apple's own format which means they can only be transferred to an iPod. iTunes is a High Street music store online, offering a wide range of music. The focus is on simplicity. Users can email friends with a sample of songs as well as create and share playlists with other users. iTunes also allows users to stream their music between five different computers, which means that music played on one computer can be played on up to five other PCs. The service however involves a single pricing model for its downloads. There are moves by some sections of the record industry to require Apple to charge for its music downloads based on their popularity, for example how often requested. These tracks would be charged for at a premium whilst tracks not in such demand would be subject to the smaller flat fee. Once again, dispute is in the offing and some commentators believe that the iTunes service gave the record industry a lifeline at a time when illegal music downloads were gaining in popularity. To impose restrictions in this way by monetizing further the popular tracks might threaten the stability of the legitimate download market and force users back to the illicit file-sharing networks.

A slightly different commercial model can be found in the online service provided by OD2 (On Demand Distribution). OD2 is Europe's most popular download service. However it simply supplies the songs and infrastructure to a number of companies such as MTV, Virgin, HMV and MSN. It does not sell tracks directly on its own website. It has a library of around 350 000 songs and uses a system of credits to purchase songs. For example a permanent download which may be copied to CD or portable device costs 100 credits. The songs are downloaded in encrypted Windows Media Audio format, which can be transferred to sixty different portable players but not including Apple's iPod. The service also allows users to generate playlists based on recommended music and those playlists can then either be downloaded or streamed to the PC.

The battle for market share in the growth of online music has also moved to the high street, with a range of high-street stores encouraging customers to buy more music on the Internet. HMV has launched its own online service which enables users to download songs from the website by transferring them to a computer file which is then loaded on to a digital music player. Indeed HMV intends to operate learning centres in its stores for new downloaders. Virgin is also preparing to offer music on the Internet and will offer a pay-as-you-go system for downloading tracks as well as a monthly subscription allowing unlimited downloading. Tesco similarly provides a music download service and at the time of publication commands a larger share of the music market than HMV.

A number of brand name ISPs are now offering a limited number of free downloads as part of their broadband package.

There is clear evidence that consumers are increasingly accessing their music from the Internet but need the encouragement of a trusted brand that can demystify the experience.

ROYALTY COLLECTION AND ONLINE MUSIC

BACKGROUND

For many years the music industry has operated with the assistance of collection societies. These are private organizations established by categories of copyright owners to administer their rights. In the UK they are supervised by Copyright Tribunal under the Copyright Designs and Patents Act 1988. Section 116(2) of that Act defines a licensing body as:

> *...a society or other organization which has as its main object, or one of its main objects, the negotiation or granting, either as owner or prospective owner of copyright or as agent for him, of copyright licences, and whose objects include the granting of licences covering works of more than one author.*

The purpose of the organizations is to offer a practical and economical service to enable their members to administer and enforce certain of their copyrights. They ensure that anyone using the copyright have the necessary licences and have paid the appropriate rate. The collection societies will collect the monies, and allocate and distribute them, for which they will charge a fee. They also have reciprocal arrangements with other societies to enable them to protect their members worldwide.

We will examine two of the collection societies in the UK. First, the Performing Right Society Limited (PRS) is the collection society for composers, songwriters and music publishers. Its role is to administer the public performance and broadcasting rights in music and lyrics. In addition it administers film synchronization rights, which is where a piece of music is used in a film production. Upon becoming a member of the PRS the copyright holder assigns their performing right and film synchronization rights to the PRS.

Next, there is the Mechanical Copyright Protection Society Limited (MCPS). This organization collectively licenses mechanical reproduction of music, which is in effect the copying of music. It negotiates and administers collective licence schemes with record companies and has both music publishers and songwriters as members. The MCPS does not require an assignment of rights, however its membership does require that the members appoint MCPS as their agent to manage and administer the mechanical copyright in this country. It charges its members a commission for administering the rights and collecting the royalties. The rate is around 9.4 to 12.5 per cent.

The PRS and the MCPS now combine many of their managerial and administration functions but they retain their separate identities.

In recent times the PRS and MCPS have sought to work effectively in the context of online music. This has proved to be a difficult task. The Internet as a means of music distribution hit the music industry fast and the very nature of the Internet and its global reach makes traditional models for administering music copyright almost unworkable. Initially the organizations did not have the mandate from all their members to grant rights for online use. In 1999 the MCPS stated that on behalf of its members it would recommend a ten pence per download rate for up to five minutes of music and two pence per minute over that. This received strong condemnation from ISPs and content providers who claimed this was too high.

At the time of writing the UK's leading online music services and the British Phonographic Industry (BPI) are mounting a legal challenge to the licence terms demanded by music publishers and composers for the use of their compositions on the Internet and on mobile devices. The seven online services, AOL, Apple iTunes, MusicNet, Napster, RealNetworks, Sony Connect and Yahoo!, are referring the problem to the Copyright Tribunal. The Copyright Tribunal is a statutory body governed by the Copyright, Designs & Patents Act 1988 and is responsible for ensuring that the terms issued by licensing bodies for the use of copyright works are reasonable. The music providers are challenging the tariff set by the MCPS-PRS Alliance for the use of musical works on the Internet and wireless devices. It is useful to review the basis of the dispute as it goes to the root of how online music services may develop.

The MCPS-PRS Alliance is a joint venture between the MCPS and PRS. The online music service providers contend that the licence the Alliance is seeking to impose for online music is unreasonable. They state that the royalty rate on a download is double the rate it charges for a song on a CD. They believe the Alliance's tariff threatens to seriously harm the development of the legal online and mobile music markets.

The publishing royalties on physical products such as CDs stand at 6.5 per cent of retail price (or 8.5 per cent of the published wholesale price). Broadcast radio rates range between 3 per cent and 5.25 per cent of net advertising revenues. The Alliance's online tariff proposals could impose a rate of 12 per cent of gross retail revenues on most online music, claim the service providers. They also state that the change in technical means of delivering music to the consumer does not warrant a sudden increase in royalties for using compositions and the higher royalties on online services place online services at an unfair commercial disadvantage. The online music services providers and the BPI further contend that the royalties to be paid to the Alliance should reflect the specific nature of the service concerned, for example permanent downloads or webcasting. In addition the level of royalties paid for similar uses of musical works offline should be factored. Another point made is the significant investments made by the online music service providers and record labels in developing legal online music services and combating the illicit music download market. The music service providers want a licensing structure for publishing rights that can allow them to stream Internet radio programming and otherwise distribute online music lawfully whilst paying a fair rate.

MCPS-PRS LICENSING SCHEME FOR THE PROVISION OF ONLINE AND MOBILE MUSIC SERVICES TO THE PUBLIC FOR PRIVATE USE

On 1 January 2005 the MCPS and PRS issued a licensing scheme for the provision of online and mobile music services to the public for private use. This scheme takes the form of a legal licence agreement or the 'Online Agreement' as it is termed by the MCPS-PRS. The scheme was scheduled to operate for one year, which reflects the fact that the market for online services is relatively new and developing rapidly. It is possible that the MCPS-PRS might consider the scheme may require introduction of new legal terms as experience dictates. The Online Agreement is granted to an online music service provider business and we will now examine some of the principal provisions in the licensing scheme operated by the MCPS-PRS.

The Online Agreement is intended to be used for online and mobile services for which music is a substantial or important part of that service. It covers the UK, Northern Ireland, the Channel Islands and the Isle of Man. It may also cover other countries as the system develops. The costs to a music business wishing to provide online music services of being granted the Online Agreement varies according to the revenue achieved by the music business. This determines the royalties payable to MCPS-PRS. Indeed the MCPS-PRS may make the grant of an Online Agreement conditional upon the provision of such financial guarantees as are reasonably necessary. This is to provide security against the risk that the members of MCPS and PRS may not receive such royalties as may be payable under the Online Agreement. This guarantee may take the form of deposits or advances. When the Online Agreement terminates any monies put up by way of guarantee will be repaid to the company which provided the guarantee.

The MCPS-PRS have set a joint royalty rate for the online exploitation of musical works at 12 per cent of the gross revenue achieved.

The term Music Service Provider is defined in the Online Agreement as:

> *...the party which, in relation to a music service, is the last party in the chain of transmission to the user actually responsible for making the music service containing repertoire works available to users, and not...a mere conduit which is only providing physical facilities for enabling or making a communication, provided that from or through this party, accurate details as to the identity of the repertoire works and the number of uses thereof and the value and the destination thereof can be obtained and audited.*

The above definition thus excludes for example ISPs who are not offering a music download service but acting as mere conduits of the facilities perhaps being offered by a company set up solely for the purpose of offering music downloads. However, recently a number of ISPs are offering music download services and in that capacity they will fall within the ambit of the MCPS-PRS licence scheme.

A Music Service is defined as meaning;

> *a service pursuant to which musical works are exploited in the following manner;*
>
> *(a) one or more copies are stored on a Data Storage Device with the intention of making such copies or other copies available to users by means of telecommunications networks (whether by wire or wireless means or a combination of both);*
>
> *In such manner that*
>
> *(b) the copy or copies reside(s) on the user's data storage device (either temporarily or permanently) or*
>
> *(c) the user is able to access the copy or copies during the delivery but no permanent copy resides on the user's data storage device or*
>
> *(d) for the avoidance of doubt, a combination of (b) and (c) above;*
>
> *but excluding:*

(i) traditional terrestrial, satellite and cable, radio and television broadcast services and near audio or near video on demand services...

A 'Data Storage Device' is for example an MP3 player, iPod or mobile phone perhaps. The licence will grant to the Music Service Provider a non-exclusive licence to do a number of things during the agreed period which the agreement is to run for: to reproduce musical works on servers within an agreed geographical territory for those servers for the purpose of transmitting the music to non-commercial users for private and domestic use only; in addition, where authorized, the temporary or permanent reproduction of the musical works on the user's iPod for example, for purely private and domestic use.

The licence will also grant a non-exclusive licence for the period of the contract, to communicate to the public musical works within, say, the UK only. The MCPS-PRS Online Agreement will also allow the Music Service Provider the opportunity to provide further services under the scope of the agreement provided they are still music services and that party can reach agreement with the MCPS-PRS as to calculation of the revised licence fee.

There are restrictions in the Online Agreement requiring that the services licensed remain music services throughout the period of the contract, and that the licensee remains a Music Service Provider.

It is possible to include audio-visual material under the licence scheme. This is defined as 'any specific presentation of musical works in synchronization or otherwise with images, whether moving or still.' It might for example be a music video production for download to a mobile phone. It could also be a live concert performance or a film of a live concert by an artist. It may be an interview with an artist, composer, producer or other person involved in the creation, performance or production of music, where these are associated with the musical work.

The Online Agreement also makes clear that the licence granted to the Music Service Provider does not allow the manufacture or distribution of physical products containing the musical works, for example the ordering of CDs via the Music Service Provider which are distributed by mail.

The manner in which payment by the Music Service Provider is to be made is also dealt with in the Agreement. Within twelve days of the end of each quarter the Music Service provider must provide to the MCPS-PRS an accurately completed self-accounting royalty statement. Within seven days thereafter the

MCPS-PRS will raise an invoice for the due amount and the Music Provider must pay that amount no later than seven days after receipt. Late payment will result in a penalty on the usual basis of three per cent above base rate from time to time on the balance outstanding.

The Music Service Provider has to notify the MCPS-PRS of its usage of the music each quarter. This information is broken down into name of the music, artist, composer, number of permanent downloads, number of temporary downloads, music duration, number of Internet streams and certain other detail which accurately reports how the Music Service Provider has used the music via its online music service. This information is known as the 'Online Reporting Data'. It must be delivered to the MCPS-PRS by the Music Service Provider in electronic format no later than one month following the end of the quarter to which the music usage information relates. In addition, the MCPS-PRS require the provider of the music services to deliver further information or documentation in its possession, power, custody or control and information of the above character not in its possession in order to enable the proper verification of the music usage and to ensure that the Music Service Provider is abiding by the terms of its licence.

This verification process is clearly central to the ability of the MCPS-PRS to monitor and account properly for all online use of music. Therefore the Online Agreement will allow for the access of the joint body to the music service for free, even when that service is offered to subscribers for a payment.

The MCPS-PRS may want to improve how they verify the music usage and they can implement new systems to achieve this. The Music Service Provider must comply provided they are given six months in which to do so.

In Chapter 7 we will examine the impact of the Data Protection Act 1998 upon the distribution of music via the Internet. Under the Online Agreement the Music Service Provider is not obliged to provide the MCPS-PRS with any information which identifies its consumer users or which otherwise constitutes 'personal data' as defined in the 1998 Act. The music usage data must still be furnished but any personal information must be removed.

There are penalties upon the Music Service Provider if it provides inaccurate usage data and this is in the form of interest payments on the royalties that have not been distributed. The interest will run from the date the MCPS-PRS should have distributed the royalties. It is important to note that the interest penalty for non-compliance is without prejudice to any other legal rights the MCPS-PRS may have against the Music Service Provider.

There are requirements upon the Music Service Provider to include certain credits as part of their service. These include:

- the logos of the MCPS and the PRS in an approved form;

- links to their respective websites;

- the name of the composer and publisher of the music;

- a notice explaining that use of the music is subject to restrictions: the notice must say that full details of those restrictions can be found at the websites of the MCPS and the PRS.

The Music Service Provider must maintain full records and make those records available for inspection upon reasonable notice both during and for twelve months following termination of the Online Agreement. These records must consist of the use of all the music offered by the provider and any income or other consideration received by or on behalf of the provider together with any supporting documentation thereto. This ability to conduct an audit of the Music Service Provider's records includes the access to its premises no more than once a year to inspect the accounting records. The MCPS-PRS representatives can then make extracts or take copies of any of the information and or documentation to do what in their opinion is necessary to comply with the Online Agreement. Once again if the audit reveals underpayment of the correct royalty fees, or if the failures to report account for at least 7.5 per cent of the music usage during the period of audit, then the Music Service Provider will have to pay the correct royalty together with interest and the MCPS-PRS's reasonable costs of such audit and verification within 28 days of the MCPS-PRS invoice.

However, if the audit reveals an overpayment of royalties by the Music Service Provider to the MCPS-PRS provided this is discovered before they have accounted to their member, the MCPS-PRS must repay the sum to the provider. No interest is paid on this sum though.

The MCPS-PRS must not disclose to a third party any information about the Music Service Provider received during the audit save that this information may be reported to the MCPS-PRS professional advisors who are under a duty to maintain confidentiality, but only if this disclosure is for purposes connected with the Online Agreement.

The Music Service Provider must take steps to ensure the security and encryption of the music it provides. Earlier in the chapter we saw how the law governs the circumvention of technical measures connected with copyright works. Under the Online Agreement the Music Service Provider must utilize industry security standards available for use in the protection of the music. In any event it must use its best commercial endeavours to prevent unauthorized copying and/or the unauthorized issuing of copies of the music by whatever technical means are practicable. It must not (and must use best commercial endeavours) to ensure that any relevant party shall not attempt to interfere with, remove or alter:

- any rights management or identifier information associated with the music;

- any technical measures associated with the music which are designed to prevent or restrict the unauthorized use of the music.

The Online Agreement may be terminated by either party by giving three months notice in writing to the other party.

However, each party may terminate the agreement immediately if the other party commits a material breach of the agreement which can be remedied but which is not remedied within 14 days after receipt of notice of such breach. Similarly, the agreement can be terminated if the party commits a material breach of the agreement which is incapable of remedy.

The MCPS-PRS have particular rights to terminate the agreement and these mainly relate to the insolvency, or threatened insolvency, of the Music Service Provider. There are though other rights in their favour alone; for example, if the Music Service Provider amends its service in such a way that the income on which a royalty is payable to the MCPS-PRS is affected in any material way. In such circumstances the MCPS-PRS can terminate the agreement. The termination would be effective on the date the service was altered. Upon termination for whatever reason all licences granted under the agreement will end and the Music Service Provider must cease all reproduction or distribution of the music via its service.

The Music Service Provider may not assign or otherwise transfer any of its rights under the Online Agreement without the written consent of both the MCPS and the PRS. This is not to say that the Music Service Provider cannot use the services of a third party when operating the music service. However, it must at all times retain complete control and direction over the provision of the licensed services to users and the MCPS-PRS must be able to audit such third party as described above.

The agreement also imposes obligations upon the Music Service Provider in relation to the music it supplies to its consumer users. These include a statement that the music may only be copied as permitted under the agreement or by applicable law (for example English law) and that no attempt must be made by users to interfere with, remove or alter:

- any rights management or identifier information associated with the music

- any technical measures associated with the music which are designed to prevent or restrict the unauthorized use of the music.

The above review of the MCPS-PRS Online Agreement offers guidance only as to certain of the obligations imposed by the scheme. The scheme is still in the very early stages of use and will undoubtedly alter as experience dictates but it can be seen that in its current form it already touches upon a number of issues known to be required under legislation pertaining to Internet music and featured elsewhere in this book.

EVIDENCE TO DATE

So, has the approach taken by the record industry to stem Internet music piracy been successful? As we have seen the strategy took the form of legal threat and in many cases court action, together with a sustained public relations campaign to warn of the perils of illicit music downloads. In 2005, 14 227 court cases were brought by the record industry in 12 countries. Against the background of the above the industry has also been actively considering new technologies to help thwart illegal file sharing.

In September 2004 the Official UK Download Chart was launched. It is compiled on the basis of actual sales of music sales from download websites in this country. The launch of the Official UK Download Chart came 52 years after the arrival of the first UK music chart or 'Hit Parade' and is seen as recognition of the reality in which music is now distributed. Some feel that the new chart will stimulate creativity where recorded music is no longer restricted to physical formats.

The latest evidence available at the time of writing seems to suggest that the battle is being won by the music industry. In the quarterly report produced by the British Phonographic Industry (BPI) in July 2005, it was announced that legitimate music download sales topped 10 million for the first half of 2005. This compares to 5.7 million for the whole of 2004. In 2004 single track downloads totalled 659 377. In 2005 the figure was 5 562 638 representing an increase of 743.6 per cent. Indeed the Internet download market appears to have jump-started the sale of singles in the UK, according to figures produced by the Official UK Chart Company. In 2004 total single sales amounted to 7 246 211 compared to 11 040 075 for 2005. This includes online sales and CD and seven-inch vinyl sales and represents a 52.4 per cent increase in sales for the year. The evidence also demonstrates that despite the huge growth in Internet downloads it would be wrong to write off physical sales of music products at this time. Record companies will need to continue to meet consumer demand whatever format the music is provided in.

Another reason perhaps for the decline in illicit music downloads is consumer fears about spyware, adware and viruses found in peer-to-peer networks.

On the matter of online music licensing, at the time of writing the European Commission is considering whether there ought to be pan-European copyright licences to improve the licensing of music copyright on the Internet.

It is felt that the absence of pan-European copyright licenses makes it difficult for new European-based online services to become established. It is said that the principal obstacle to the growth of legitimate online content services in the EU is the difficulty in securing attractive content for online exploitation. In particular, the present structures for cross-border collective management of music copyright (which were developed for the analogue environment), prevent music from fulfilling its unique potential as a driver for online content services. The European Commission believes that only music has the real potential to kick-start online content services in Europe. The online music services targeted by the review include simulcasts, which are the simultaneous broadcast of programmes or events across more than one medium. In addition, webcasting and streaming, downloading or an online on-demand service are included. So too are music services provided to mobile telephones. The basis is that all of these services can be enjoyed across Europe and as a consequence their copyright needs to be cleared throughout Europe. The Commission has concluded that entirely new structures for cross-border collective management of copyright are required. The most effective model to achieve this is for copyright holders to authorize a collecting society of their choice to manage their works across the entire EU. The copyright holder's freedom to choose any collecting society in the EU would create a powerful incentive for those societies to provide optimal services to all their rightholders, irrespective of their location, thereby enhancing cross-border royalty payments.

Another development underway at the time of publication is the UK Government's plans for extending the copyright term for pop songs in order to bring the UK into line with the US. At present, UK copyright in a literary, musical, artistic or dramatic work lasts for 70 years after the death of the author, while sound recordings and broadcasts are protected for 50 years after the year of publication. The consequence of this for example is that the sound recording copyright owned by record companies in major 1960s hits by the Beatles and the Rolling Stones has less than 10 years to run – 40 years less than would apply if the US copyright laws were applicable in this country. The Government is considering the change on the basis that an extension would raise more money for the music industry, which can be ploughed back into new talent. There is some concern by some artists that the rule would prevent sample and remix fragments of classic songs.

Whilst the distribution of music via the Internet has made huge strides in the last year or so it is also clear that there is still a large amount of work to do in establishing a framework for online royalty collection.

CHECKLIST

- Ensure that the music business understands fully the 'making available right' and that the music website fulfils the requirements of the Copyright and Related Rights Regulations 2003.

- Consider whether adoption of the Creative Commons Licence is appropriate to the music business online activity.

- Check that the rules on royalty collection for online music are understood.

CHAPTER 6

Online Marketing of Music and Merchandise

PRIVACY AND ELECTRONIC COMMUNICATIONS (EC DIRECTIVE) REGULATIONS 2003

INTRODUCTION

The development of apparatus in the telecommunications sector in recent years is tremendous. In particular mobile phones have evolved to the extent that they no longer merely serve as voice data instruments permitting telephone conversations from wherever there exists a service. The equipment now enables photographs to be taken and instantly emailed to other mobile subscribers, limited form of Internet access and, with the arrival of 3G services, video downloads and broadcast material direct to the phone. They are a modern-day marvel.

It did not take long for those in the marketing industry to recognize the potential for mobile phones as highly sophisticated marketing tools. The attraction rests in the ability to contact the subscriber directly, wherever they might be. Mobile phones and handheld devices offer all the benefits of the Internet without the major hurdle of being restricted to sitting in front of a computer. The attraction of offering music via mobile apparatus is heightened by the uptake of 3G which not only speeds up mobile access to the Internet but also provides handsets with faster processors and, crucially, larger screens that will make for example watching music videos more appealing to a wider audience. The interest in using mobile phones as a means of selling goods and services is made more acute with the possibility of location-based services. For example, a music retailer based in a shopping mall or perhaps exhibiting at a concert can send a text or email to the mobile phone of those people in the vicinity of the shop or stand offering a discount on CDs for the first 100 visitors. The message is only received by the subscriber if they are within a defined radius but one can see how powerful the sales potential is by the use of such sophisticated technology.

Most artist fans searching for information or merchandise relating to their favourite band do not search the Internet under the name of the band's record company. It is likely the fan cares not which label the artist is signed to. They will search using the name of the band or artist. Record company websites tended in the early days of the Internet to be principally corporate information sites providing details for the benefit of other companies. Today, record company websites are far more orientated towards a magazine format offering latest news on their roster of artists. Usually the website will be linked to another website perhaps owned by the artist's management. Another likely link might be to another organization providing related services or merchandise in relation to the artist. In Chapter 11 we examine how a strategic link between a record company and a computer games developer offering an online game designed around a particular band would be regulated by a formal Linking agreement.

Music businesses now provide a vast array of deals on their websites designed to support the promotion of their artists. The attraction of the Internet as a medium for such activity is the ability to interact with the website visitor in a manner hitherto not possible. Indeed music websites can provide record companies with information about their artist's fan base, which they could not gather by other means. Websites can serve as points of contact by which personal data about the fan can be ascertained. This might include age, gender and location including country of residence. We examine in Chapter 7 how music companies must abide by the requirements of the Data Protection Act 1998 when they gather and maintain such information.

Websites offer the company an ability to interact with the fans in real time and to offer time-specific deals to those fans who can enter online competitions, communicate with their favourite artists live and purchase merchandise on a special offer for, say, a limited number of hours. Record companies tend to use their websites as a means of offering additional, otherwise unobtainable information to fans. When one considers the degree of sophistication to which a music business can market and promote its bands using the Internet, one can understand why the music industry places great emphasis on their websites. Record companies therefore will want to either own or control artist websites and domain names.

Branding of artists has never been more popular and commercially attractive. There has been huge interest in television formats which allow the public to vote for would-be pop stars and effectively create music careers almost overnight. These interactive television programmes are always supported by websites which also offer the ability to vote in the contest. The websites can also offer a glimpse of the inside story and behind-the-scenes activity of the contestants as the competition develops. Given that many of these artists will enjoy fame and sell records for a comparatively short period the need to maximize earnings through as many media as possible is clear. The Internet provides this possibility and the interactive nature and convergence with television has spawned a new genre of programming. The success of this branding frenzy rests also with the deployment of as many media technology outlets as possible. The increasingly sophisticated mobile phone and its appeal to the youth market offers just such an outlet.

The growth in mobile marketing, despite a slow start, is now apparent and its relationship to music promotion is clear. First, mobile subscriptions are approaching 100 per cent saturation in the UK and will exceed that as individuals begin to use more than one mobile phone. The apparatus themselves have become fashion items and have obvious appeal to a youth market. The same age demographic tend to be those who purchase music singles and albums and, as fans of particular artists, have a demand for merchandise which promotes the artist. The phones now have colour-screen capacity offering the ability to view video content. The music industry appreciates that with clever data collection they can deliver real-time video content direct to a fan's mobile phone based on their age, gender and musical preference. The key to this marketing nirvana lies on the collection and retention of that data.

In many ways the reaction to mobile marketing is defined by generation. For many people who did not grow up with mobile phones the thought of being bombarded with marketing messages wherever they might happen to be is appalling. However, to a generation which does not know life without mobile communication it is probably a natural state of affairs and as consumers with spending power they have no objection to the trend.

Nonetheless regulators soon appreciated that there must be sensible control over the use of people's personal information and the way a company could obtain, and then commence transmission to, someone's mobile phone number. The whole question once again turns on the issue of data protection and in order to protect the privacy of mobile subscribers it would prove necessary to introduce a set of laws which would make clear what is and what is not acceptable.

Given the significant adoption of mobile phone technology by the music industry it is important to review the laws which must be adhered to in this area. In this section, we make frequent use of examples and for the purpose of illustration characterize the business as a music company or music business. This term could include a record company or promoter or any other business associated with the music world and as such will be used as a generic term.

As we will see in Chapter 7 the Data Protection Act 1998 is the legislation in the UK which governs the use of personally identifiable information relating to individuals. The principles contained in that Act must still be met by a music business wishing to develop a marketing campaign targeted at its email and mobile phone consumer database. However, in addition to the Act the music company must also abide by the provisions of the Privacy and Electronic Communications (EC Directive) Regulations 2003.

In many ways these Regulations and the need for them highlight the problem lawmakers face in the world where media technology develops so quickly. In 1999 for example, hardly an age ago and certainly not ancient by legislative standards, there were regulations introduced to control the unfettered use of telephone numbers by businesses wishing to sell to consumers. Those regulations were called Telecommunications (Data Protection and Privacy) Regulations 1999. In the short period following their adoption email use and mobile phone adoption was such that it was clearly necessary to revisit the issue of control and come up with a new set of rules more suited to the reality of the marketplace. The result, following a good deal of consultation with industry and consumer groups alike, is the Privacy and Electronic Communications (EC Directive) Regulations 2003.

The Regulations came into effect in the UK on 11 December 2003. It is important to emphasize that given their nature as Regulations they are common to the rest of the EU. As such however, their ambit extends only throughout the member states and they do not and cannot govern activity generated outside the EU.

In our review of the Regulations it is important to make clear that we are talking about voice data telephone calls, SMS text messages and email and other electronic messaging.

Regulation 4 of the new Regulations make clear that they do not relieve a person of any obligations under the Data Protection Act 1998.

TRAFFIC DATA

Regulations 7 and 8 set out certain restrictions on the processing of traffic data relating to a subscriber or user by a telecommunications provider. When one considers the issue it can be appreciated that the study of actual user data can reveal how the subscriber uses their mobile phone. This of course is useful to mobile phone service providers so they can market appropriate tariffs to their subscribers. It would also be of interest to those marketing other services, such as third-party companies wishing to sell other goods and services.

Traffic data is defined as 'any data processed for the purpose of the conveyance of a communication or an electronic communications network or for the billing in respect of that communication'. *Public communications provider* is defined as 'a provider of a public electronic communications network or a public electronic communications service'.

If we consider traffic data from the perspective of a music business wishing to market and promote its artists' music via a mobile phone network in order to get to potential consumer purchasers the following explanation is helpful.

Regulation 7 says that traffic data relating to a subscriber or user may be processed and stored by a provider of a public electronic communications service in certain circumstances. Remember, we are not talking about third-party organizations here, only the phone service provider.

They may process and store the data if:

- it is for the purpose of marketing electronic communications services;

- it is for the provision of value-added services to that subscriber;

- the subscriber has given their consent to the processing or storage;

- the processing or storage is done only for the duration necessary for the marketing of their services or provision of their value-added services.

The phone subscriber must be told by the company about the kind of information of which the traffic data will consist and the duration of such processing before their consent is given.

The processing considered above can only be done for the following purposes:

- the management of billing or traffic;

- customer enquiries;

- the prevention or detection of fraud;

- the marketing of electronic communications services; or

- the provision of value-added services.

So, the sophistication which traffic data afford a marketeer is restricted only to the phone service provider. It cannot be made available to, for example, a music company wishing to tailor its marketing message according to how their artist fan base actually use their mobile phones.

Regulation 10 is a provision relevant to music businesses who obtain the mobile number of their target consumer by following the appropriate procedure detailed later in this section. It says that the provider of a public electronic communications service shall provide users originating a call with a simple means to prevent presentation of the identity of the calling line on the connected line as respects that call. Thus, the calling music business could take up this facility so that the consumer would not necessarily know the identity of the company. This service must be provided free by the phone service provider company.

LOCATION DATA

Let us now look at the matter of location data. We stated earlier that the use of location-based services by a music company was possible.

Suppose the music company wishes to provide value-added services to the mobile phone consumer via a network and it strikes an agreement with the network provider to offer certain services or merchandise. Which rules must the music company and the phone company provider adhere to when offering such a service?

The Regulations say at 14(2) that location data relating to a user may only be processed where that user cannot be identified from such data or where necessary for the provision of a value-added service with the consent of that user or subscriber.

Before obtaining the consent of the subscriber the phone company must provide the following information to the subscriber:

- the types of location data that will be processed;

- the purposes and duration of the processing of the data;

- whether the data will be transmitted to a third party for the purpose of providing the value-added service.

The subscriber can withdraw his consent at any time free of charge. The said processing of the location data can only be carried out by

- the public communications provider in question;

- the third party (such as the music company) providing the value-added service in question; or

- a person acting under the authority of either of the above.

Suppose the music business wants to set up an automated calling system to contact its target consumers. The Regulations also set out how this process must be conducted. Regulation 19(2) states that the phone subscriber must have previously given his or her consent to such communications being sent.

UNSOLICITED TEXT MESSAGING FOR DIRECT MARKETING PURPOSES

We now turn to the rules which must be followed strictly if a music business wishes to contact consumers with a view to marketing or promoting the artist material. First, let us consider this process assuming the music company wishes to do this on an unsolicited basis using, for example, the mobile phone number of the subscriber.

The Regulations provide for two mechanisms by which the consumer can ensure no unsolicited phone calls are made to their number. First, the person may have notified the music company that no such calls should be made to that number. Second, the consumer may have registered their phone number with the Telephone Preference Service. This is a register maintained by OFCOM which contains the numbers of individuals who do not wish to receive any unsolicited phone calls.

Provided the consumer has not then either notified the music company of their objection to marketing calls or has registered with the Telephone Preference Service, it is possible for the company to make unsolicited calls to that individual. Remember, the definition of 'calls' includes both voice data and SMS text messages.

So, the rules for making speech calls to a target consumer or indeed sending them a text message are clear. However, with convergence of technology many mobile phones also have the capacity to send and receive email communications. The Regulations also contain rules concerning use of email for marketing purposes.

There was a great deal of consultation by the UK Government before the Regulations were introduced. The concern was to ensure that the fair activities of the marketing community were properly balanced with the legitimate needs of consumers to maintain privacy. It must be understood that the Regulations only apply in the context of business-to-consumer relationships. That is, they apply solely to situations where a business, such as a music company, wishes to make unsolicited telephone calls or send unsolicited emails to a target consumer. The Regulations do not apply to the situation where a business wishes to market its services to another business. This was largely due to the fact that businesses expect to be marketed to and to impose a bar on marketing calls and emails would run counter to the spirit of enterprise. The Government, however, made it clear that if the evidence over the next few years pointed to business-to-business unsolicited communications becoming a significant menace then further regulation would be considered with a view to combating the problem.

The other point to emphasize is that these laws can only address the problem of unsolicited messages if they originate from within the EU. The rules of course do provide a framework for music businesses in terms of how they must go about marketing their merchandise and services using electronic communications. The Regulations have been successful in controlling what was fast becoming a major problem. They cannot however govern music businesses based outside the EU. Therefore such businesses can still send unsolicited communications to consumers and of course other businesses without restriction. This is why many readers will doubtless receive several emails a day from businesses based for example in the US.

There are exceptions to the general bar on sending unsolicited emails as a music business to consumers.

If the business can demonstrate that one of the following conditions has been satisfied then it will not be deemed to have infringed the Regulations. Regulation 22(3) states that:

> *A person may send or instigate the sending of electronic mail for the purposes of direct marketing where:*
>
> *(a) that person has obtained the contact details of the recipient of that electronic mail in the course of the sale or negotiations for the sale of a product or service to that recipient;*
>
> *(b) the direct marketing is in respect of that person's similar products and services only; and*
>
> *(c) the recipient has been given a simple means of refusing (free of charge except for the costs of the transmission of the refusal) the use of his contact details for the purposes of such direct marketing, at the time that the details were initially collected, and, where he did not initially refuse the use of the details, at the time of each subsequent communication.*

These exceptions allow for a degree of flexibility on the part of a music business which intends to market its merchandise. For example, (a) might be satisfied if the consumer has previously given their contact details to the company as part of a promotional offer or competition. It might be that the music company offered a prize of concert tickets inviting people to enter the competition and asking they complete their address details. Any contact details thus obtained would permit the company to commence sending emails to those individuals without infringing the Regulations.

The second exception, (b), is also fairly wide. In the case of a supermarket selling a wide range of products it might be difficult for them to start marketing music CDs to their consumer database when those consumers have only previously purchased groceries. However, in the case of a music business it might be that it has previously sold music CDs to its consumers but now wishes to offer film DVDs or perhaps a music-track download service. Such offers would amount to similar goods or services and therefore the company would not infringe the Regulations.

The third exception deals with where a consumer notified their willingness to receive future marketing communications. The individual has to opt in to the receipt of such messages. In the past, a marketing department could regard an individual's silence as acceptance. Thus, the company could draft a response form for the consumer to complete which required the consumer to tick a box to indicate their objection to receiving material in the future (opt out). If the consumer did not tick that box the company was entitled to assume that consent had been granted and they could continue to send material. Now, the Regulations require the consumer to tick expressly that they have no objection to receiving marketing communications.

If a music company wishes to instigate a marketing campaign using electronic communications it should then follow the above procedures. It should also state clearly the precise means by which it may market its merchandise or services to the target consumer in the future. Thus, if it intends to send SMS text messages to the individual's phone this must be made clear. If it wants to send emails, this must be clarified.

One interesting point of note is that, as we have said, the Regulations only apply to individuals. However, the definition of individuals also includes 'an unincorporated body of such individuals' which could include a legal partnership.

Regulation 23 prohibits the sending of communications by means of email for the purposes of direct marketing where the identity of the person on whose behalf the communication is made has been disguised or concealed or an address to which requests for such communications to cease may be sent has not been provided.

A music business cannot seek to exclude a consumer's rights under the Regulations by contractual term. So for example, in the website terms and conditions (Chapter 3) the company could not include a clause which informed their online consumer that they could expect to receive future marketing communications without offering that person the ability to register their express consent.

There are penalties which will be imposed on a music business which seeks to infringe the Regulations. Regulation 30 allows a claim for damages to be brought in respect of contraventions of the Regulations. It is the person receiving the messages who can bring legal proceedings. It is a defence by the music company that the company can prove it took 'such care as in all the circumstances was reasonably required to comply with the relevant requirement'.

The Regulations also add an obligation on those companies who wish to use *cookies* or other similar tracking devices to notify their use to their online consumer. A cookie is an electronic tag which permits website operators to identify the buying habits of their online consumers. They allow for very sophisticated marketing. The Regulations do not forbid the use of such technology in a website but the music company must include a clause in its website terms and conditions notifying the visitor to the website that the website uses cookies for these purposes.

For a music business the dawn of mobile marketing combines the wide reach of television with the precision of direct marketing and the tracking potential of the Internet. Some in the new media sphere believe that the mobile phone could become one of the most important media for advertisers and marketeers. In the initial phase of mobile marketing some major brands ran mobile campaigns which were usually one-off pilots with little long-term commitment. More recently companies have taken the medium more seriously and the music industry is an obvious participant. The potential for music to be marketed via mobile phones has been ushered in by two principal factors: first, fast networks and high functionality phones; second, the sheer ubiquity and importance of the mobile phone among consumers. Indeed some research suggests that people were more willing to do without television than their mobile phones.

The devices of course do more than facilitate voice calls. In 2004, 26 billion text messages were sent in the UK. With the ability to send content-rich messages made possible by 3G, record companies now appreciate that mobiles must become a part of their promotional portfolio. Strategic mobile marketing is now seen as part of their communication strategy. In addition, phone operators can enter into the music services domain by offering, for example, music shows via their network. Such services have already begun to have an impact on the youth market for phones. The possibilities for delivering appealing media content to mobiles are tremendous. However, at the time of writing there are limits to the technology and thus its attraction to the music industry. For any technology to become mass market it has to be universal. At present 3G is not. Handset penetration has a significant way to go and interoperability is also acting as an inertia to growth.

Music businesses are integrating mobile phones into their content. For example it is now common for a record company to offer music ringtones of tracks featured on a new album release. The user simply sends a text message to a specified number code and for around £3 they can obtain a polyphonic ringtone.

It is useful to consider how a music company might go about marketing its artists' music and supporting merchandise by the use of mobile phones. As we have seen, the telephone service provider can use the traffic and billing data it holds about its subscribers for the purpose of marketing further services to them. It cannot however release that data to a third-party company. It can however release the mobile phone number of a subscriber to a third-party company such as a music business where the telephone service company has included a clause in its network access contract with the subscriber. That clause might state that the company is entitled to release numbers to third-party companies with a view to those companies sending marketing messages.

If the telephone company has included this notification then the music business might acquire (for a fee) that database of mobile phone numbers. However, the music business would then have to send an initial message to the subscriber stating that they intend to send marketing messages in the future and the means by which those messages will be sent. This is known as a Data Protection Notice. The subscriber must then expressly signify their agreement to receiving those messages. This acceptance might be given by visiting the music company's website to register consent. Provided the subscriber does give consent in this way the music business can commence marketing its products and services to the mobile phone subscriber. The subscriber can though refuse their consent at any time and if so notified the company must cease transmission of material or face legal penalties.

CHECKLIST

The 2003 Regulations changed the previous rules in the following ways:

- They replace the previous definitions for telecommunications services and networks with new definitions for electronic communications and services to ensure technological neutrality and clarify the position of email and use of the Internet.

- They enable the provision of value-added services based on location and traffic data, subject to the consent of subscribers (for example, location-based advertising to mobile phone users).

- They remove the possibility for a subscriber to be charged for exercising the right not to appear in public directories.

- They introduce new information and consent requirements on entries in publicly available directories, including a requirement that subscribers are informed of all the usage possibilities of publicly available directories, for example reverse searching from a telephone number in order to obtain a name and address.

- They extend controls on unsolicited direct marketing to all forms of electronic communications including unsolicited commercial email (spam) and SMS to mobile telephones.

- They introduce controls on the use of cookies on websites.

CHAPTER 7

Collecting Online Data about Music-Buying Consumers

PRIVACY CONSIDERATIONS AND ONLINE MUSIC

The Internet's greatest attraction is that it is an open environment. One area which offers huge opportunity for a music business is the increasingly sophisticated means by which personal information about the consumer can be obtained. The richness of the content of this data and how it may be measured is simply incredible and was not possible only a few years ago. To ensure the success of many online music applications, whether it is the offer of physical music CDs and other merchandise over the Internet, or the making available of online music downloads, it is important the company can target its users properly. However, the Internet does not exist in a legal vacuum. In the EU, at least, it resides in a heavily regulated data protection regime. In this chapter we will examine why privacy laws have huge significance in relation to the Internet and mobile telephone use by music companies.

The sheer wealth and diversity of its content encourages the immediate, though often transient, review of a host of published data. There are legitimate concerns by consumers over marketeers buying and selling their personal information. The rise of e-commerce has sparked increasing fears, due to the ease with which all types of sensitive data may be gathered, copied, shared and misused via the Internet.

It is vital that a music business understands how it may operate safely and adhere to the legal protection afforded to individuals in the EU. Moreover, given the pan-national nature of the Internet, the company needs to know how it can process personal information in a way which does not fall foul of the data protection regime of other countries.

These problems are particularly acute for music companies with an international reach. In addition to possible fines there is a risk of negative publicity for breaching data protection laws. No company can afford to ignore the issues.

It is necessary to examine the basis of data protection principles as they apply within the EU and to consider how they relate to a music company's use of the Internet and mobile communications apparatus. In addition, the rules for transfer of data from the UK (and indeed from any country in the EU) to a country outside the EU will be explained.

It is fair to say that the EU has one of the most stringent data protection regimes in the world. Some feel that there is an absence of connection between this restricted approach and the realities of the global nature of the Internet.

The information-gathering ability of companies has caused concerns over invasion of citizens' rights for many years. In most countries, the unlawful processing of personal data represents a violation of fundamental human rights.

In the UK, company directors are personally liable for the accuracy of their organization's databases. Individuals can sue not merely for financial loss directly resulting from inaccurate or wrongly disclosed data, but for any breach of data law and resultant distress.

To view the significance of the data protection rules to a music company's existing or planned online operations one need only consider that a commercial website which is run by a music business may well sell music in physical or digital download form as well as other merchandise. The information superhighway collects, processes and transfers a prodigious amount of personal data. When purchasing from a website the online customer will of necessity disclose their home address, contact details, credit card information and other personal information. Confidence that the music business will maintain that data responsibly is vital. For example, a music company may wish to develop new methods of earning revenue for its artists. Recording artists of course earn revenue by touring. However, there are moves by some artists to provide virtual touring as a means of record promotion. These are webcasts of the artists' live performances over the Internet. By streaming concerts the music webcast can be made available on a series of websites contemporaneously by simulcast. With the increased adoption of broadband in many homes the quality of these webcasts is improving all the time. The saving to the artist of course is that they can record the concert in a studio perhaps developed for this purpose. The concert could be broadcast on the artist's own website. Whether these webcasts were sponsored by another company as part of a sponsorship package, paid for by the fans on a pay-per-view basis or offered free as a promotional activity by the music company, there is a need to capture personal information of the consumer base. Clearly, if a music company wanted to provide regular webcasts of this kind it would want to gather data about its artists' fans, particularly their email addresses so that they might be notified of future webcasts and offered the chance to purchase tickets to the concerts online.

The Internet permits music companies to monitor profiles and information provided directly by the music fan. The process of tracking every click the fan makes on the Internet and leaving behind cookies on their computers to help the system remember each consumer is hugely valuable. Companies can gather a startling amount of personal information with which to sell consumers music merchandise and services. The vast majority of commercial websites are dependent on cookies to customize the site to users' preferences; without them, sites become almost unusable.

Illustration of the technology for example lies in a purchase of a music CD on Amazon. In time, the site will begin to suggest new purchases each time the consumer visits, based on the buying pattern that individual has established.

The argument in favour of online marketing is that it helps consumers find the right products efficiently and with convenience. There are controls on the use of cookies contained within the Privacy and Electronic Communications Regulations 2003 as we have seen in Chapter 6. However, since many browsers allow users to block cookies and to delete them from their PCs a criticism has been levelled at Europe. It is suggested that user awareness about the use of cookies is the preferred approach rather than legal constraint. The contrary view is that such ability creates many new ways for highly personal data to be misused or stolen.

DATA PROTECTION ACT 1998

In the UK the law which governs the processing of personal data is embodied in the Data Protection Act 1998 (the Act). This Act came into force on 1 March 2000. It replaced the Data Protection Act 1984 and it implements the principles of EU Directive 95/46/EC.

In 1995 the European Parliament and Council issued the EU Directive on Data Protection (95/46/EC). The Directive sought to protect individuals with regard to the processing of personal data and free movement of such data. The Directive led to the introduction of the 1998 Act, which is more extensive than the 1984 legislation. Whilst the Act sets forth the overall legal framework, much of the detail is contained in secondary legislation.

The most significant difference to previous legislation is the new definition of *processing*. This is defined as 'obtaining, recording or holding the information or data or carrying out any operation or set of operations on the information or data'.

Thus, for music businesses, particularly those which make extensive use of the Internet or indeed IT generally to run their business processes, the Act imposes a significant compliance programme. The Act applies in the following circumstances:

1.   if the music business is 'established' in the UK, that is, it is ordinarily resident, a UK limited company, partnership or unincorporated business: in addition, the Act applies if that business has an office, branch or agency which carries on any activity in the UK;

2.   if the music business is not established in the UK but uses equipment in UK for processing data;

3.   if data is exported to the music business from the UK.

As is the case with much of the law relating to online music strategies featured in this book, there is correspondent legislation in place throughout the EU subject only to minor variation.

The information covered by the legislation is *personal data*, that is, data relating to a living individual who can be identified directly or indirectly. Employees, suppliers, customers and business contacts all fall within the definition.

DATA PROTECTION PRINCIPLES

The 1998 Act and related EU regulation set out eight principles which organizations must follow:

> *1. All personal data which is held must be processed fairly and lawfully. It must not be processed unless one of the conditions at Schedule 2 is met. More stringent conditions apply to the processing of sensitive personal data. These are set out in Schedule 3 to the 1998 Act. The Act defines 'sensitive personal data' as 'personal data consisting of information as*

to a data subject's racial or ethnic origin, political opinions, religious beliefs, or other beliefs of a similar nature, membership of a trade union, physical or mental health or condition, sexual life, or commission or alleged commission or proceedings in relation to any of them.

Processing sensitive data will only be legitimate if the data subject has given their 'explicit consent'. If sensitive personal data is used, at least one condition at schedule (3) must also be met. It is clear that personal data will not considered to be processed 'fairly' unless certain information is provided, or made readily available to the individual concerned.

The information to be given to data subjects must include the identity of the data controller, the purposes for which the data is intended to be processed and any further information which is necessary having regard to the specific circumstances in which the data is to be processed, to enable processing in respect of the data subject to be fair. Where data is obtained directly from the data subject, the requisite information should normally be provided at, or be made available from, the time of data collection.

2. Personal data shall only be obtained for one or more specified and lawful purpose. It should not be further processed in a manner incompatible with that purpose.

3. Personal data must be adequate, relevant and not excessive in relation to the purpose for which it is processed. Whilst an online enquirer may be willing, in the course of a transaction, to give a music business a great deal of personal information, that business has a duty to protect enquirers from themselves and their generosity. Clearly this has implications for data collection by a music business via the Internet. Many websites require regular visitors to register before gaining access. It is very important that the music business make clear precisely why non-essential questions are being asked and whether a response is optional. For example, capturing an email address may be necessary for the provision of a particular service, whereas collecting information about gender, marital status, income and age may be irrelevant or excessive.

4. Personal data must be accurate and kept up to date where necessary.

5. Personal data processed for any purpose shall not be kept for longer than is necessary for that purpose.

6. Personal data must be processed in accordance with the rights of data subjects under the Act.

7. Appropriate technological and organizational measures will be taken against unauthorized or unlawful processing of personal data. Such action will also be taken in the case of accidental loss, destruction or damage to personal data.

This principle needs to be considered carefully by the music business. If the music business uses a data processor such as an ISP or other third party which processes data on its behalf – for example by hosting the website – it will be in breach of this seventh principle unless both of the following criteria are satisfied:

(i) the processor provides sufficient guarantees in respect of the technical and organizational security measures governing the processing to be carried out, and the music business takes reasonable steps to ensure compliance with those measures;

(ii) the processing is governed by a written contract requiring the processor to act only as instructed by the controller and to comply with security obligations equivalent to those imposed in the controller. In the context of the Internet, the music business will therefore need to ensure it has appropriate and properly documented contractual arrangements in place with, amongst others, its ISP and website hosters.

EXPORTING DATA FROM THE UK TO A COUNTRY OUTSIDE THE EU

Eighth data protection principle and transborder data flows

There is one facet of privacy legislation which causes some confusion and can easily be overlooked by a music business, in particular by those with an international dimension to their business. The problem is particularly manifest in the context of electronic communications. The ease with which information can be passed around the globe at the press of a button is contributing to the widespread oversight of the laws which control export of personal data. In many ways the enabling technology which permits the easy transfer of information is to blame in that the effortless process does not prompt an investigation of the law which controls the action.

The Act introduces a new principle. It prohibits the transfer of personal data outside the EU unless there is an adequate level of protection in the receiving country, or the individual concerned has consented to the transfer.

There are a number of factors which determine the adequacy of legislation in other legal jurisdictions. These include the purpose for which data will be used and the risk involved. There is a problem: few countries outside the EU in fact operate adequate data protection provisions. Since the Internet permits the global transfer of data, monitoring of data flow is difficult thereby exacerbating the problem. First it is necessary to consider the broad ambit of the Act.

A music business might infringe the law relating to export of personal information in ways quite common to everyday business operation: for example the use of information collected as a result of online ordering to send offers of merchandise to existing online customers worldwide. This is the kind of activity which is undertaken daily by music businesses in this country.

The legal basis of control lies within the Act. Section 4 (4) of the Act provides that:

> ...it shall be the duty of a data controller to comply with the data protection principles in relation to all personal data with respect to which he is the data controller.

It is the eighth principle which governs transborder data flows which is relevant here. The Eighth Principle states:

> 8. Personal data shall not be transferred to a country or territory outside the European Economic Area unless that country or territory ensures an adequate level of protection for the rights and freedoms of data subjects in relation to the processing of personal data.

The European Economic Area consists of the 25 EU member states together with Iceland, Liechtenstein and Norway. The Eighth Principle prohibits the transfer of personal data to any country or territory outside the EEA, a so-called 'third country' unless the third country in question ensures this 'adequate level of protection for the rights and freedoms of data subjects' for transfers of their personal data to such countries. The Act does not define 'transfer' but the ordinary meaning of the word is transmission from one place or person to another. It is important to appreciate that transfer does not mean the same as mere transit. Thus, the fact the electronic transfer of for example a music-buying consumer database may be routed through a third country on its way from the UK to another EEA country does not bring such transfer within the ambit of the Eighth Principle unless some substantive processing operation was being conducted upon the personal data in the third country in question. A company can fall within the ambit of the restriction very easily without realizing it. If information is provided by, for example, the marketing manager in a music business in the UK over the telephone to his counterpart in a third country who then enters the information on a computer, the legislation will be breached. Another problem area would be mass data transfers from computer to computer using telecommunications systems.

'Processing' is widely defined by the Act and includes the obtaining, using, recording or holding of information, as well as adaptation or retrieval and disclosure of data. In effect, the obligations and principles apply to almost any use or collection of data regarding an individual. Certain information is classified as 'sensitive', and there are additional obligations in relation to sensitive personal data. If the music business wished to include data regarding its consumer's racial or ethnic origin, political beliefs, religious beliefs or sex life these are regarded as sensitive. A UK music business intending to transfer data to a third country must assess the question of adequacy. To most companies, these will appear convoluted. In assessing adequacy the data controller in the music business is required to make a judgement as to whether the level of protection afforded by all the circumstances of the case is commensurate with the potential of personal risks to the rights and freedoms of its consumer database (the data subjects) in relation to the processing of personal data. There are detailed guidelines which assist all companies in making the assessment and in adhering to good practice. These are too numerous to detail for the purposes of this book. There are however several forms of international transfer which have been identified by the Confederation of British Industry (CBI) where it may be possible for exporting controllers to approach the adequacy test with a strong presumption in favour of adequacy in terms of assessing the risk involved in the transfer. In the context of a music business these might include:

- transfers to a third-party processor who remains under the control of the exporting data controller in the music business;

- transfers within an international or multi-national music business or group of music businesses where an internal agreement, policy or code is more appropriate than a potentially large number of contracts;

- transfers between the providers of professional services such as lawyers or accountants whose clients' affairs are international in scope;

- transfers which amount to a licence for use and probably a rental payment in respect of personal data used, for instance, in direct marketing; and

- transfers which constitute a sale of data to a third party where there is no continuing relationship either with the data subject or the purchaser.

All member states in the EU must take the measures necessary to prevent any transfer of data of the same type to the country in question where the European Commission finds no adequate level of data protection exists. Of particular relevance to a music business is the market in the US for artists. However, the US is deemed to be a country where no adequate level of protection exists. So if the music business wishes to transfer data from the UK to the US, two methods of data transfer have been developed: the so-called 'safe harbor' and the EU model clauses. There are a number of alternative options.

First, signing up to the US Safe Harbor Privacy Principles will legitimize transfers to the US.

A second route to compliance is by putting in place contracts between the exporting music business and the importing business. This is a common route to compliance within a corporate group. However, the standard terms which must be included may not prove palatable to many music businesses, given how weighted they are in favour of the individual consumer.

A third option to addressing transfer may be developing as a variant to a contract on the European Commission's approved terms. In the UK at least, it is open to a music business to adopt a policy on privacy compliance which is applicable throughout the company. This policy may be sufficient to address transfer issues provided the policy is binding. This means some form of external dispute resolution mechanism. However, this can be drafted more favourably to the music business than the equivalent provisions in the European Commission's approved terms.

US SAFE HARBOR PROCEDURE

US Safe Harbor was the result of five years of negotiation between the US Department of Commerce and the European Commission adopting a decision regarding safe harbor principles. The principles came into effect on 1 November 2000. It is intended to ensure the adequate level of privacy necessary to allow the transfer of data from the EU to the USA. Essentially Safe Harbor provides a set of privacy principles which replicate the data protection principles enshrined by the EU data protection regime. These include:

- notice (of intended use and intended recipients, and of how to limit use and make enquiries and complaints)

- choice (both opting out and opting in)

- security

- data integrity

- data subject access rights

- enforcement mechanisms (including effective follow-up procedures).

It is important to emphasize that Safe Harbor only applies between the EU and the US. It is a fair to say that the reaction of most businesses in the US to the Safe Harbor principles has been unenthusiastic. Comparatively few US corporations have notified the Department of Commerce that they adhere to them. Notable corporations that have registered include Microsoft and Hewlett Packard.

EU MODEL CLAUSES

As we have seen, the Safe Harbor principles only extend to transfers of data between the EU and the US. The European Commission also released a separate scheme for any transfer out of the EU. A set of what are called 'model clauses' enable parties to transfer data outside the EU to other parties located in countries, falling short of the adequate level of protection by means of a private contractual arrangement.

Both parties must execute a fixed, prescribed agreement distinct from any other commercial agreement that they may be entering into. Thus, whatever the nature of the commercial deal being struck between music businesses in say the UK and the US, the parties must enter into a separate legal agreement which incorporates the prescribed model clauses. A good deal of experience has been gained since the model clauses were first introduced. For example, a number of business groups such as the International Chambers of Commerce (ICC) and the Confederation of British Industry (CBI) wanted to adapt the clauses to make them more commercially relevant. As a result in December 2004 the EU issued new model clauses to facilitate data flows from the EU. The model clauses ensure that data controllers are able to perform data transfers globally under a single set of data protection rules. The new model clauses are set out below for reference but specific legal advice must be taken to establish whether in fact the clauses apply to the circumstances the music business may operate under. In the specimen clauses set out, we have assumed a transfer of data between a UK record company, perhaps of its consumer database, to a US-based joint-venture record company.

It will be appreciated that the issue of transferring data from the UK to any country outside the EU is complex and it is sufficient for the purposes of this book to highlight that a music business wishing to export data must be mindful of the law and take specific legal advice on how to proceed.

Specimen EU model clauses

Standard Contractual Clauses For The Transfer Of Personal Data From The Community To Third Countries (controller to controller transfers)

Data Transfer Agreement

Between

A Record Company UK Ltd

Whose registered office is at.............., United Kingdom.

Hereinafter 'data exporter'

And

American Record Company Inc

Whose principal place of business is at.............., California, United States.

Hereinafter 'data importer'

Each a 'party'; together 'the parties'

Definitions

For the purposes of the clauses:

a. 'personal data', 'special categories of data/sensitive data', 'process/ processing', 'controller', 'processor', 'data subject' and 'supervisory authority/authority' shall have the same meaning as in *Directive* 95/46/EC of 24 October 1995 (whereby 'the authority' shall mean the competent data protection authority in the territory in which the data exporter is established);

b. the 'data exporter' shall mean the controller who transfers the personal data;

c. 'the data importer' shall mean the controller who agrees to receive from the data exporter personal data for further processing in accordance with the terms of these clauses and who is not subject to a third country's system ensuring adequate protection;

d. 'clauses' shall mean these contractual clauses, which are a freestanding document that does not incorporate commercial business terms established by the parties under separate commercial arrangements.

The details of the transfer (as well as the personal data covered) are specified in Annex B, which forms an integral part of the clauses.

I. Obligations of the data exporter

The data exporter warrants and undertakes that:

a. The personal data have been collected, processed and transferred in accordance with the laws applicable to the data exporter.

b. It has used reasonable efforts to determine that the data importer is able to satisfy its legal obligations under these clauses.

c. It will provide the importer, when so requested, with copies of relevant data protection laws or references to them (where relevant, and not including legal advice) of the country in which the data exporter is established.

d. It will respond to enquiries from data subjects and the authority concerning processing of the personal data by the data importer, unless the parties have agreed that the data importer will so respond, in which case the data exporter will still respond to the extent reasonably possible and with the information reasonably available to it if the data importer is unwilling or unable to respond. Responses will be made within a reasonable time.

e.   It will make available, upon request, a copy of the clauses to data subjects who are third party beneficiaries under clause III, unless the clauses contain confidential information, in which case it may remove such information. Where information is removed, the data exporter shall inform data subjects in writing of the reason for removal and of their right to draw the removal to the attention of the authority. However, the data exporter shall abide by a decision of the authority regarding access to the full text of the clauses by data subjects, as long as data subjects have agreed to respect the confidentiality of the confidential information removed. The data exporter shall also provide a copy of the clauses to the authority where required.

II. Obligations of the data importer

The data importer warrants and undertakes that:

a.   It will have in place appropriate technical and organizational measures to protect the personal data against accidental or unlawful destruction or accidental loss, alteration, unauthorized disclosure or access, and which provide a level of security appropriate to the risk represented by the processing and the nature of the data to be protected.

b.   It will have in place procedures so that any third party it authorizes to have access to the personal data, including processors, will respect and maintain the confidentiality and security of the personal data. Any person acting under the authority of the data importer, including a data processor, shall be obligated to process the personal data only on instructions from the data importer. This provision does not apply to persons authorized or required by law or regulation to have access to the personal data.

c.   It has no reason to believe, at the time of entering into these clauses, in the existence of any local laws that would have a substantial adverse effect on the guarantees provided for under these clauses, and it will inform the data exporter (which will pass such notification on to the authority where required) if it becomes aware of any such laws.

d.　It will process the personal data for purposes described in Annex B, and has the legal authority to give the warranties and fulfil the undertakings set out in these clauses.

e.　It will identify to the data exporter a contact point within its organization authorized to respond to enquiries concerning processing of the personal data, and it will cooperate in good faith with the data exporter, the data subject and the authority concerning all such enquiries within a reasonable time. In case of legal dissolution of the data exporter, or if the parties have so agreed, the data importer will assume responsibility for compliance with the provisions of clause I(e).

f.　At the request of the data exporter, it will provide the data exporter with evidence of financial resources sufficient to fulfil its responsibilities under the clause III (which may include insurance coverage).

g.　Upon reasonable request of the data exporter, it will submit its data processing facilities, data files and documentation needed for processing to reviewing, auditing and/or certifying by the data exporter (or any independent or impartial inspection agents or auditors, selected by the data exporter and not reasonably objected to by the data importer) to ascertain compliance with the warranties and undertakings in these clauses, with reasonable notice and during regular business hours. The requests will be subject to any necessary consent or approval from a regulatory or supervisory authority within the country of the data importer, which consent or approval the data importer will attempt to obtain in a timely fashion.

h.　It will process the personal data, at its option, in accordance with:

(i) the data protection laws of the country in which the data exporter is established, or

(ii) the relevant provisions of any Commission decision pursuant to Article 25(6) of Directive 95/46/EC, where the data importer complies with the relevant provisions of such an authorization or decision and is based in a country to which such an authorization or decision pertains, but is not covered by such authorization or decision for the purposes of the transfer(s) of the personal data, or

(iii) the data processing principles set forth in Annex A.

Data importer to indicate which option it selects:_____

Initials of data importer:_____

j.   It will not disclose or transfer the personal data to a third data controller located outside the European Economic Area (EEA) unless it notifies the data exporter about the transfer and

    i.   the third party data controller processes the personal data in accordance with a Commission decision finding that a third country provides adequate protection, or

    ii.   the third party data controller becomes a signatory to these clauses or another data transfer agreement approved by a competent authority in the EU, or

    iii.   data subjects have been given the opportunity to object, after having been informed of the purposes of the transfer, the categories of recipients and the fact that the countries to which data is exported may have different data protection standards, or

    iv.   with regard to onward transfers of sensitive data, data subjects have given their unambiguous consent to the onward transfer.

III. Liability and third party rights

a.   Each party shall be liable to the other parties for damages it causes by any breach of these clauses. Liability as between the parties is limited to actual damage suffered. Punitive damages (i.e. damages intended to punish a party for its outrageous conduct) are specifically excluded. Each party shall be liable to data subjects for damages it causes by any breach of third party rights under these clauses. This does not affect the liability of the data exporter under its data protection law.

b.   The parties agree that a data subject shall have the right to enforce as a third party beneficiary this clause and clauses I(b), I(d), I(e),

II(a), II(c), II(d), II(e), II(h), II(i), III(a), V, VI(d) and VII against the data importer or the data exporter, for their respective breach of their contractual obligations, with regard to his personal data, and accept jurisdiction for this purpose in the data exporter's country of establishment. In cases involving allegations of breach by the data importer, the data subject must first request the data exporter to take appropriate action to enforce his rights against the data importer; if the data exporter does not take such action within a reasonable period (which under normal circumstances would be one month), the data subject may then enforce his rights against the data importer directly. A data subject is entitled to proceed against a data exporter that has failed to use reasonable efforts to determine that the data importer is able to satisfy its legal obligations under these clauses (the data exporter shall have the burden to prove that it took reasonable efforts).

IV. Law applicable to the clauses

These clauses shall be governed by the law of the country in which the data exporter is established, with the exception of the laws and regulations relating to processing of the personal data by the data importer under clause II(h), which shall apply only if so selected by the data importer under that clause.

V. Resolution of disputes with data subjects or the authority

a. In the event of a dispute or claim brought by a data subject or the authority concerning the processing of the personal data against either or both of the parties, the parties will inform each other about any such disputes or claims, and will cooperate with a view to settling them amicably in a timely fashion.

b. The parties agree to respond to any generally available non-binding mediation procedure initiated by a data subject or by the authority. If they do participate in the proceedings, the parties may elect to do so remotely (such as by telephone or other electronic means). The parties also agree to consider participating in any other arbitration, mediation or other dispute resolution proceedings developed for data protection disputes.

c. Each party shall abide by a decision of a competent court of the data exporter's country of establishment or of the authority which is final and against which no further appeal is possible.

VI. Termination

a.   In the event that the data importer is in breach of its obligations under these clauses, then the data exporter may temporarily suspend the transfer of personal data to the data importer until the breach or the contract is terminated.

b.   In the event that:

    i.   the transfer of personal data to the data importer has been temporarily suspended by the data exporter for longer than one month pursuant to paragraph (a);

    ii.   compliance by the data importer with these clauses would put it in breach of its legal or regulatory obligations in the country of import;

    iii.   the data importer is in substantial or persistent breach of any warranties or undertakings given by it under these clauses;

    iv.   a final decision against which no further appeal is possible of a competent court of the data exporter's country of establishment or of the authority rules that there has been a breach of the clauses by the data importer or the data exporter; or

    v.   a petition is presented for the administration or winding up of the data importer, whether in its personal or business capacity, which petition is not dismissed within the applicable period for such dismissal under applicable law; a winding up order is made; a receiver is appointed over any of its assets; a trustee in bankruptcy is appointed, if the data importer is an individual; a company voluntary arrangement is commenced by it; or any equivalent event in any jurisdiction occurs.

then the data exporter, without prejudice to any other rights it may have against the data importer, shall be entitled to terminate these clauses, in which case the authority shall be informed where required. In cases covered by (i), (ii), or (iv) above the data importer may also terminate these clauses.

c.   Either party may terminate these clauses if (i) any Commission positive adequacy decision under Article 25(6) of Directive 95/46/ EC (or any superseding text) is issued in relation to the country (or a sector thereof) to which the data is transferred and processed by the data importer, or (ii) Directive 95/46/EC (or any superseding text) becomes directly applicable in such country.

d. The parties agree that the termination of these clauses at any time, in any circumstances and for whatever reason (except for termination under clause VI(c)) does not exempt them from the obligations and/ or conditions under the clauses as regards the processing of the personal data transferred.

VII. Variation of these clauses

The parties may not modify these clauses except to update any information in Annex B, in which case they will inform the authority where required. This does not preclude the parties from adding additional commercial clauses where required.

VIII. Description of the transfer

The details of the transfer and of the personal data are specified in Annex B. The parties agree that Annex B may contain confidential business information which they will not disclose to third parties, except as required by law or in response to a competent regulatory or governmental agency, or as required under clause I(e). The parties may execute additional annexes to cover additional transfers, which will be submitted to the authority where required. Annex B may, in the alternative, be drafted to cover multiple transfers.

Dated:_____

An American Record Company Inc

FOR DATA IMPORTER

....

....

....

A Record Company UK Ltd

FOR DATA EXPORTER

....

....

....

Annex A

DATA PROCESSING PRINCIPLES

1. Purpose limitation: Personal data may be processed and subsequently used or further communicated only for purposes described in Annex B or subsequently authorized by the data subject.

2. Data quality and proportionality: Personal data must be accurate and, where necessary, kept up to date. The personal data must be adequate, relevant and not excessive in relation to the purposes for which they are transferred and further processed.

3. Transparency: Data subjects must be provided with information necessary to ensure fair processing (such as information about the purposes of processing and about the transfer), unless such information has already been given by the data exporter.

4. Security and confidentiality: Technical and organizational security measures must be taken by the data controller that are appropriate to the risks, such as against accidental or unlawful destruction or accidental loss, alteration, unauthorized disclosure or access, presented by the processing. Any person acting under the authority of the data controller, including a processor, must not process the data except on instructions from the data controller.

5. Rights of access, rectification, deletion and objection: As provided in Article 12 of Directive 95/46/EC, data subjects must, whether directly or via a third party, be provided with the personal information about them that an organization holds, except for requests which are manifestly abusive, based on unreasonable intervals or their number or repetitive or systematic nature, or for which access need not be granted under the law of the country of the data exporter. Provided that the authority has given its prior approval, access need also not be granted when doing so would be likely to seriously harm the interests of the data importer or other organizations dealing with the data importer and such interests are not overridden by the interests for fundamental rights and freedoms of the data subject. The sources of the personal data need not be identified when this is not possible by reasonable efforts, or where the rights of persons other than the individual would be violated. Data subjects must be able to have the personal information about them rectified, amended or deleted where it is inaccurate or processed against these principles. If there are compelling grounds to doubt the legitimacy of the request, the organization may require further justifications before proceeding to rectification, amendment or deletion. Notification of any rectification, amendment or deletion to third parties to whom the data have been disclosed need not be made when this involves a disproportionate effort. A data subject must also be able to object to the processing of the personal data relating to him if there are compelling legitimate grounds relating to his particular situation. The burden of proof for any refusal rests on the data importer and the data subject may always challenge a refusal before the authority.

6. Sensitive data: The data importer shall take such additional measures (eg relating to security) as are necessary to protect such sensitive data in accordance with its obligations under clause II.

7.   Data used for marketing purposes: Where data are processed for the purposes of direct marketing, effective procedures should exists allowing the data subject at any time to 'opt out' from having his data used for such purposes.

8.   Automated decisions: For purposes hereof, 'automated decision' shall mean a decision by the data exporter or the data importer which produces legal effects concerning a data subject or significantly affects a data subject and which is based solely on automated processing of personal data intended to evaluate certain personal aspects relating to him, such as his performance at work, creditworthiness, reliability, conduct, etc. The data importer shall not make any automated decisions concerning data subjects except when:

(a) (i) such decisions are made by the data importer in entering into or performing a contract with the data subject, and

(ii) the data subject is given an opportunity to discuss the results of a relevant automated decision with a representative of the parties making such decision or otherwise to make representations to that parties.

Or

(b) where otherwise provided by the law of the data exporter.

Annex B

DESCRIPTION OF THE TRANSFER

(To be completed by the parties)

Data Subjects

The personal data transferred concern the following categories of data subjects:

....

....

Purposes of the transfer(s)

The transfer is made for the following purposes:

....

....

Categories of data

The personal data transferred concern the following categories of data:

....

....

Recipients

The personal data transferred may be disclosed only to the following recipients or categories of recipients:

....

....

Sensitive data (if appropriate)

The personal data transferred concern the following categories of sensitive data:

....

....

Data protection registration information of data exporter (where applicable)

....

....

Additional useful information (storage limits
and other relevant information)

....

....

Contact points for data protection enquiries

Data importer   Data exporter

....

....

RIGHTS OF INDIVIDUALS AGAINST AN ONLINE MUSIC BUSINESS

Individuals (or 'data subjects') have extensive rights under the Act and a music business must comply. The consumer may write to the music business and ask to be supplied with a description, purposes and any disclosures made of or a copy of any personal data being held. The music business must respond to that request within 40 days on receipt of a single fee (the fee levels are set by regulations and may alter). The consumer also has the right to prevent processing likely to cause damage. In addition, the consumer has the right to claim compensation from the music business if it contravenes certain requirements of the Act. In the case of inaccurate data, the consumer can apply to the court for correction, blocking, erasure or destruction. Consumers must also be notified when data is being collected and be told how it may be used and who is collecting it.

PENALTIES FOR A MUSIC BUSINESS FOR BREACHING THE DATA PROTECTION ACT

It is a criminal offence not to register where a music business holds appropriate data. A larger threat is that of having to pay compensation where damage has been caused by the loss, unauthorized destruction or disclosure of personal data. There is of course also the potential for damaging adverse publicity resulting from such action.

DATABASE RIGHT AND THE MUSIC BUSINESS

We have seen how the rights of individuals are protected by the data protection regime in the EU and what a music business must do to abide by the Data Protection Act.

We will now examine what protection the music business has in the database it has sought to compile and concerning which it has gone to great lengths to meet the requirements of the Data Protection Act. Clearly the database which the music business compiles could have enormous commercial value and will likely be the result of considerable effort over a long period of time on the part of that business. We will review the law which governs databases as works which attract financial value.

On 1 January 1998 the Copyright and Rights in Databases Regulations 1997 came into force in this country. The aim was to improve the protection given to databases and harmonize such protection throughout the EU.

A database is defined by Regulation 6 as:

> ...*a collection of independent works, data or other materials which (a) are arranged in a systematic or methodical way, and (b) are individually accessible by electronic or other means.*

The definition captures hard-copy databases but it also applies to online collections.

A database right arises automatically, in common with copyright. However, there are two prerequisites to be met before the right can exist: in the first place, Regulation 13(1) states that there must have been 'a substantial investment in obtaining, verifying or presenting the contents of the database'. Next, the maker or if it was complied jointly, one of its makers, must be a national or if a company, incorporated in the European Economic Area. The 'maker' is defined by Regulation 14(1) as:

> ...*the person who takes the initiative in obtaining, verifying or presenting the contents of a database and assumes the risk of investing in that obtaining, verification or presentation.*

It is the maker who will usually be the first owner of the database right. It is important to point out that if the maker is an employee, then it is the employer who will be the first owner.

Database right lasts for 15 years from the end of the calendar year in which it was either completed or first made available to the public. It is also possible that a substantial change to the contents of a database will result in this 15-year period commencing once again from that time as being considered substantially a new investment. In effect therefore it is entirely possible that databases will enjoy a rolling period of protection which could extend for many years beyond first compilation.

Regulation 16 grants the owner the right to prevent the extraction and/or re-utilization of the whole or a substantial part of the contents of the database. 'Extraction' is defined as the permanent or temporary transfer of any contents of a database to another medium by any means or in any form. 'Re-utilization' means making those contents available to the public by any means.

As with copyright law there are a number of defences available to the person or company who is alleged to have infringed the database of an owner. These include 'insubstantiality'. This is defined as meaning 'substantial in terms of quantity or quality or a combination of both'. However, it is possible to infringe an owner's database right by a series of what might be insubstantial copying acts. Another defence is that of 'lawful user' in relation to the database. This would include an express licence granted by the owner or possibly an implied licence. This might be where the owner has not actually given consent for the use of its database but its conduct might lead a court to conclude that the right can be deemed to have been granted.

The music business should ensure that the arrangement of its data is systematic or methodical and that the data is individually accessible. In addition, it should maintain a record of the investment it has made in obtaining, verifying or presenting its database. This record must be kept safely. This will be necessary if the music business is ever called upon to prove its investment was substantial and thus attract the protection of the Regulations. As noted the continued additions to a database could mean that its period of protection runs well beyond the 15-year right.

CHECKLIST

- Ensure that the music business is registered under the Data Protection Act 1998 if the website is collecting personal information about individual fans.

- The music website must display a full privacy policy and the website legal terms and conditions must contain full information on the individual's rights in relation to their personal data.

- Ensure that the music business understands the eight data protection principles under the Data Protection Act 1998.

- If the music business will be transferring personal data outside the EU then it must use the model clauses or sign up to the US Safe Harbor if the transfer is to the US.

CHAPTER 8

Distance Selling Regulations and Online Music and Merchandise Sales

The sale of music CDs and DVDs by retailers over the Internet is now commonplace. Items of this kind are low risk in the eyes of the purchaser in that they are probably already aware of the product and its content and the modest value of the unit means they are more willing to consider an online purchase. Other physical merchandise which might be offered for sale online by a music business may similarly be of slight consequence or the item may be more difficult for the consumer to assess until they actually receive the goods. In any event there is a good deal of scope for a music business to make available products connected with its artists by means of the Internet. These products can be distributed to a worldwide audience if desired and with modern logistics most can be dispatched and delivered to the consumer within a matter of days anywhere across the globe.

In 2005 the artist Robbie Williams launched an online subscription service transforming him into a retailer and cashing in on intellectual property ranging from images to live footage and interviews. The website is thus a full commercial business rather than a marketing strategy. Subscribers have access to a library of over 1000 images and exclusive behind-the-scenes video clips together with every Robbie Williams video.

However, there are important legal considerations which a music business must be aware of before offering merchandise for sale via the Internet. These rules only apply to businesses based within the EU where that business supplies to a consumer online purchaser. The laws we are about to consider do not apply where merchandise is sold online to other businesses.

The background to the consumer protection legislation forming the subject of this chapter lies in the EU's desire to protect consumers who enter into contracts for the purchase of goods or services away from business premises. It was considered that people should have the opportunity to examine the goods or services being offered, as they would have done if buying in a shop. Thus, a cooling-off period would be desirable. The legislative tool by which contracts concluded at a distance are governed is the Consumer Protection (Contracts Concluded by Means of Distance Selling) Regulations 2000. In fact these Regulations were not written with the Internet in mind, although by definition an Internet sale is a distance contract. They therefore apply to online sales of goods and services by businesses based in the EU to consumers similarly based anywhere in the EU. The Regulations are commonly referred to as the 'Distance Selling Regulations'.

CONSUMER PROTECTION (CONTRACTS CONCLUDED BY MEANS OF DISTANCE COMMUNICATION) REGULATIONS 2000

The Distance Selling Directive was adopted by the European Parliament and Council in May 1997 and has been implemented by the UK by the Consumer Protection (Contracts Concluded by Means of Distance Communication) Regulation 2000 (SI 2000 No. 2334).

These Regulations came into force in this country on 31 October 2000. However, on 6 April 2005, the Consumer Protection (Distance Selling) (Amendments) Regulations 2005 also came into force. These change the original Regulations in relation to certain issues.

AIM OF THE REGULATIONS

The Regulations are intended to protect consumers against some of the risks involved in distance selling. Online consumers are granted certain rights where they enter into contracts which have been concluded over the Internet.

In essence, even where a contract has been concluded, in some instances an online consumer can extract themselves from the contract without penalty.

DISTANCE CONTRACT

'Distance contracts' are defined broadly as:

> *Any contract concerning goods or services concluded between a supplier and consumer under an organised distance sales or service provision scheme run by the supplier, who, for the purpose of the contract, makes*

exclusive use of one or means of distance communication up to and including the moment at which the contract is concluded.

The key to the applicability of the Regulations is a contract where the supplier and the consumer do not come face to face prior to the conclusion of the contract. They provide protection for consumers in the UK shopping for goods and services by telephone, mail order, fax, interactive TV and the Internet.

The Regulations harmonize laws in all member states so that all European consumers have equality of access to goods and services in other member states.

INFORMATION TO BE PROVIDED BY A MUSIC BUSINESS TO ITS ONLINE CUSTOMERS

The Regulations specify that prior to the conclusion of any distance contract a consumer must be provided with the following information. The music business is required to provide certain clear and comprehensible information in good time before the Internet sale is made. This detail should be included on the company's website and includes the following:

1. The music company's identity must be supplied. If the contract requires payment in advance, the company's address should be displayed on the website. We have seen in Chapter 4 that in any event under the E-commerce Regulations 2002 a music business which sells merchandise or services via its website must provide this detail.

2. The principal characteristics of the company's goods or services should be specified.

3. All prices including taxes should be specified.

4. Delivery costs must be clear, as should all payment arrangements.

5. The right of the online consumer to withdraw must be specified.

6. Any costs of using the Internet as a means of distance communication must be highlighted.

CONTRACTS FALLING OUTSIDE THE REGULATIONS

Certain contracts are excluded from the operation of the Regulations. These include contracts for the supply of foodstuffs, beverages or other goods intended for everyday consumption supplied to the home of the consumer, to their residence, or to their workplace.

Thus, Internet sales of perhaps artist-branded foodstuffs such as sweets will not be subject to the Regulations because of the perishable nature of the goods concerned.

Audio or video recordings or computer software which the music business consumer has unsealed are excluded.

In addition, contracts for the provision of accommodation, transport, catering or leisure services, where the supplier undertakes, when the contract is concluded, to provide these services on a specific date or within a specific period are excluded. For example, hotel and travel bookings are not covered by the Regulations. So, if the music business makes available via its website a facility for fans to make bookings for tickets for their favourite band combined with travel and overnight hotel stay, such an offer will not fall under the Regulations.

Other exceptions to the general right to withdraw include contracts:

a) for the provision of services if performance has begun, with the consumer's agreement, before the end of seven working days;

b) for the supply of goods or services, the price of which is dependent on fluctuations in financial markets that cannot be controlled by the music business;

c) for the supply of goods made to the consumer's specifications or clearly personalized or which, by reason of their nature, cannot be returned or are liable to deteriorate or expire rapidly. For example, a music retailer might via its website make an exclusive offer to the first thousand visitors to its website for a personalized item of merchandise. Such merchandise falls outside the scope of the Regulations;

d) for the supply of newspapers, periodicals and magazines;

e) for gaming and lottery services.

A review of the exceptions listed above should enable a music business to establish whether its services offered online fall outside the Regulations and thus do not allow its online customers to withdraw from the contract.

CONSUMER PROTECTION (DISTANCE SELLING) (AMENDMENTS) REGULATIONS 2005

The principal aim of the changes to the Distance Selling Regulations is to make the right of cancellation clearer in the context of the provision of services. Prior to the amendments there was a requirement on a business to inform the consumer in writing or another durable medium, before the contract is made, that they will not be able to cancel the contract once performance of the services has begun with their agreement. This created problems for some businesses who receive orders over the phone for services which consumers want straight away or within a couple of days. In such cases compliance with the Regulations was impracticable or unduly costly if information needed to be faxed or sent by post or even courier urgently. It also meant that performance of the services could well be delayed.

To overcome these problems the right to cancel has been amended. For a music business the new provisions could be important to understand if the business is offering some form of service and this service is available to consumers not only via the website but perhaps by telephone request. This is most likely to arise by the use of mobile phones where the music consumer is required to call in to take advantage of an offer of services and the contract is effectively concluded via that phone call. We will therefore now examine the effect of the changes in that context.

The music business is no longer required to inform the consumer, prior to the conclusion of a contract for services, that they will not be able to cancel once performance has begun with their agreement. Under the changed provision, the music business must, in such cases, provide the consumer with information as to how the right to cancel may be affected if the consumer agrees to performance beginning less than seven working days after the contract was concluded. This information must be provided prior to or in good time during the performance of the contract.

Next, there is no right to cancel where the music business providing services gives information as to how the right to cancel may be affected, as set out above, before performance of those services begins and the consumer agrees to such performance beginning before the end of the cooling-off period.

Where the music business providing services gives information as to how the right to cancel may be affected as set out above, in good time during the performance of the services, there is a right to cancel even if the consumer agrees to performance beginning within the seven working days of the contract being concluded, but the cooling-off period begins when the consumer receives the information and ends seven working days later or when performance is completed (whichever is sooner).

The music business can still exclude the right to cancel by including terms in its contracts with consumers to the effect that the consumer agrees that the services will begin before the end of the cooling-off period. In order to do this, the music business will need to inform consumers about the loss of the right to cancel prior to the contract being concluded unless agreement is sought from the consumer otherwise than as part of the contract.

Where, however, the music business is happy not to exclude the right to cancel, information concerning the right to cancel can be provided in good time during the performance of the services rather than prior to the conclusion of the contract.

The consumer's right to cancel is lost when the performance of the services is completed. This may prove difficult though where there is not 'good time' to provide information about the cancellation right before the services are completed. Where the information is not provided in good time but the services have been substantially performed or are completed, the right of cancellation is preserved.

PROPOSED DRAFT GUIDANCE FOR THE DISTANCE SELLING REGULATIONS

At the time of writing the Office of Fair Trading and the Department of Trade and Industry have launched a consultation on joint draft guidance that will update and inform those selling online of their duties under the Distance Selling Regulations. The draft guidance will seek to clarify some ambiguities after the Regulations came into force. It is felt there are still some areas of confusion. One area of uncertainty is CD, DVD and software sales over the Internet. The current guidance suggests that if the consumer has broken the seal on such products when they are received, the goods cannot then be returned to the music business who supplied them online. However, this may create a problem for consumers who cannot see software licence terms without breaking a seal or running a disk.

There is also a need for clarity in the case of download sales such as music or mobile ringtones. It is recognized that those selling such items are providing a service and not selling goods. The current guidance confirms that the exception to the right to cancel will apply if the music business has the consumer's agreement to start the service before the end of the seven-day cancellation period and it has provided the consumer with the required information before starting the service. This information must include a statement that the consumer's cancellation rights will end as soon as the service begins. The question of exactly when a service does begin also needs to be made clearer. The current guidance states that preparatory work to providing a service such as the user setting up an account with the music business cannot be regarded as carrying out a service. This of course impacts on the right of a music business to say that the provision of a service has begun and therefore cannot be cancelled.

It is clear what the online music business must do on the matter of refunds for the supply of, for example, CDs DVDs or other merchandise. If a customer cancels an order for merchandise by email but fails to return the item, the music business cannot delay making the refund. The refund must be made as soon as possible after the customer cancels and within 30 days at the latest. Interestingly, even if the consumer returns merchandise which is damaged they still do not lose their right to cancel under the Regulations. Clearly the music business still has a right of action against its online customer for failing to take reasonable care of the merchandise, but this could prove difficult and hardly worth the time and money involved in the effort.

There is also the question of how much the refund should be to the music business online customer. If the music business supplies merchandise such as artist tour promotional clothes the full price paid for the clothes including the cost of delivery must be refunded. However, what if the music business also offers other services such as gift wrapping or express delivery of the item? It is recommended that the music business service should be structured so that there is one contract for the supply of goods where a refund is available and another for a supply of services that is non-refundable.

CHECKLIST

- If the music business is selling physical merchandise online to consumers in the EU then the Distance Selling Regulations apply.

- Certain products and services are excluded from the Regulations including foodstuffs and online hotel or flight bookings.

CHAPTER 9

Paying for Internet Music Distribution

Most transactions conducted over the Internet at present use existing payment products such as credit cards. However, as online commerce has grown, new easy methods of payment are being introduced. In large part these are targeted at products which may be fashionable and whose appeal lies in immediacy of access.

The primary concern with all payments made online has been one of security. Whilst more people than ever are comfortable with the Internet and with buying items online using their credit cards the fact remains that fear of fraud remains a significant barrier to e-commerce.

In this section we will consider the relationship of the Internet and the laws of money.

ELECTRONIC PAYMENT SYSTEMS

The fact that electronic payments to acquire merchandise or services over the Internet involve electronic transfers is of course not unique. Most retailers employ debit card transactions which are also electronic transactions.

The inertia which acts on adoption of electronic payment over the Internet is not merely predicated upon concerns over the security of the transaction between payer and payee. The identity of the payer and irrevocability of the payment are also factors, as is universal acceptance of the type of electronic payment.

CREDIT CARDS

Most business-to-consumer transactions conducted online are effected by credit card payments. The purchaser inserts their credit card details by completing an online form which is then transmitted to the seller over the Internet. The transmission is usually encrypted which provides additional security.

There are a number of attractions for a music business to utilize this most common of payment methods. From the consumer's point of view, credit cards are familiar. They need not enter into additional agreements and there are no currency conversion problems. Moreover, the consumer buying online using their credit card has the protection of the Consumer Credit Act 1974, placing them in a better position than by paying in cash.

For example, Section 75 of the Consumer Credit Act applies to transactions where any single item is worth between £100 and £30 000. If there is no pre-existing agreement between the card issuer and the supplier, the cardholder has enhanced legal rights. They can pursue either the supplier or the card issuer itself for misrepresentation or breach of contract. This is because the Act makes the card supplier jointly and severally liable. From the perspective of the music business selling merchandise or services, using credit cards also has advantages. There is no need for specialist equipment to be installed by potential customers and thus purchasing online is easier for Internet users.

The principle disadvantage to the music business as a vendor is the need for it to enter into a merchant account with a card issuer. This is necessary to allow the business to accept credit cards. Another factor to consider is of course the transactions costs associated with credit card payments.

Internet card payment transactions are classed as card not present (CNP) transactions. As the cardholder (and the card) is not physically with the Internet music business at the time of the transaction, it is not possible for the business to check details or the customer's signature.

There are risks associated with CNP transactions which the music business must understand and make a commercial judgement upon. Primarily, whenever the business concludes an Internet transaction, there is no guarantee of payment. If the online customer should query the transaction at a later date or any discrepancies arise, the card issuer may resort to a chargeback to recover funds from the music business. Unfortunately, fraud is common where the cardholder is not present.

There are a number of problems which the music business may encounter in the context of CNP transactions. The customer may claim that the card was used fraudulently or deny the transaction. They might maintain that the card has been stolen or claim that the card number has been used without their authority. Finally, they may say that they never received the merchandise or argue that it is defective, not as described or not of merchantable quality. In each of these cases a chargeback may result. It is therefore very important that the music business encourage its staff to record details accurately and to be vigilant.

The company should always keep a record of the details of the transaction. This is because it may need to provide the credit card merchant with such details if the online customer subsequently queries the transaction with their card company. The customer might query the date of transaction or their card number. The music business should retain records for at least three years.

There exists a tripartite relationship between the music business, the card issuer and the online customer. In this country case law has established that using a credit card creates three distinct legal contracts. The first is the contract of supply between the music business and its card-holding online customer. Second is the contract between the music business and the card-issuing company. The card issuer undertakes to honour the card by paying the music business upon presentation of the sales voucher. Thirdly, there is the contract between the card-issuing company and the Internet customer.

The card-holding customer undertakes to reimburse the card issuer for all payments made or liabilities incurred by the card issuer to the music business as a result of the customer's use of their credit card. It can be seen that in each contract, each party is involved in two of the three contracts but none is party to all three.

A cardholder who purchases by credit card completes that contract with the music business as supplier of the merchandise or services. The music business must then look to the card issuer for payment. The effect is that if the card issuer fails to pay the music business, perhaps because the issuer has become insolvent, the music business cannot then seek payment from its online customer.

The most significant risk to the music business which adopts a credit card facility is one which pertains to any retailer who subscribes to a credit card merchant agreement. Section 83 of the Consumer Credit Act 1974 states that generally a consumer cannot be made liable for the misuse of their credit card by a third party. Usually, the credit card agreement makes the cardholder liable for the first £50 while the card is not in their possession until the card issuer receives notification of the card's loss.

Nonetheless, the Internet customer using their card can, within a certain time limit, dispute a transaction that may be the result of theft, fraud or error. If the card issuer accepts that payment should not proceed a 'chargeback' occurs. The music business may not only have to repay the disputed sums but also a processing fee. Given that on any one transaction the majority of Internet purchases are for modest values such as music downloads or ringtone acquisitions, the processing fee might exceed the transaction value.

As all transactions which the music business completes online will be conducted in this way, it might prove more difficult for the business to obtain a merchant account. The card issuer will usually require the music business to provide additional eligibility information: this might mean the music business having to disclose its volume of business, credit history, cost of merchandise, debt load, length of time in business and refund policies to the card issuer.

In addition, if the product or services can actually be delivered electronically they can be denied more easily. Where physical merchandise is supplied, the music business can usually prove that the goods have been delivered to its customer's address. The Internet customer cannot therefore argue that the transaction did not take place. They can probably only allege that the merchandise was not what they ordered or is defective. So, it can be seen that if the music business is delivering online, while the cost of reproducing and delivering the merchandise might be lower, it may suffer the payment of numerous chargebacks with attendant processing fees. If this were multiplied, the music business might even lose its merchant account.

SECURE ELECTRONIC TRANSACTIONS (SET)

The Secure Electronic Payment Protocol is based on encryption technology. Its aim is to provide an agreed security standard for use in making payments over the Internet. Its intention is to maintain the privacy of Internet transactions. In addition, it addresses the needs for the identity of the payer to be verified so that their instructions could be relied upon.

Secure Electronic Transactions work as follows. Two separate keys, one public and one private, are used to encode and decode the message. The public one used encrypts the message using a complex formula. The message is then transmitted over the Internet in an encrypted form. The public key is published in a directory and therefore can be assessed by third parties. However, the message sent can only be read using the private key, and this will only be known to the receiver.

The identity of the sender is established by the use of digital certificates. These verify that the music business concerned has the authority to use the public key in which the message sent is encrypted. The certificates are in the form of small electronic documents issued by certification authorities. The use of these certificates is coupled with the use of a digital signature which operates by encrypting the message in a cryptographic algorithm called a hash function. The encryption is made using the sender's private key. The sender's public key is then used by a recipient to reconstitute the hash and is compared with other hashes generated by the sender for authenticity. This process of authenticating identity is rather like checking a handwritten signature on a cheque against a cheque card.

It is important for the music business to ensure non-repudiation by the sender. A traditional payment method such as a cheque can be cancelled at any point before it is cashed. The only way to achieve irrevocability with online payment is to take one further step. It is necessary for the music business to incorporate into its website terms and conditions an express stipulation that any instructions/payments are irrevocable once sent unless proved not to be authentic.

MICROPAYMENT SYSTEMS

The Internet is the perfect medium for accessing low-cost items which can be downloaded easily and for which transaction values often do not exceed more than a few pounds. Many of these are directed toward the youth market. Examples in the music industry include mobile phone ringtone downloads, artist screensavers, music video downloads and SMS bulletins with the latest news about bands or concerts. Such transactions have a huge effect on e-commerce and are highly successful. However, they do not warrant the use of credit cards and their attraction is the immediacy of their offer. To meet the demand for such items a new form of online payment geared towards low-cost purchases has developed. It is known as micropayment.

One example in the UK is the telecommunications giant BT's *click&buy* service. This system permits the user to buy items or services for modest sums online. The total is then added to the user's fixed telephone bill at the end of the month, which records all transactions made online whereby the user's account was operated. Micropayment systems are a breakthrough as they overcome the security concerns which exist with online payment. In addition, they permit those under 16 to make purchases over the Internet and via mobile phone against a pre-determined monthly spend set by the parent.

We will now briefly examine the typical provisions found in a contract between a music business wishing to offer for example ringtones or artist music videos for viewing on mobile phones, and the micropayment service provider company.

TYPICAL PROVISIONS IN MICROPAYMENT CONTRACTS

It is almost certain to be the case that the music company will have to operate on the basis of the standard terms and conditions which the micropayment provider issues. The music company will not have any scope for revision of those terms.

The business model we will examine consists of the micropayment service provider, the music company wishing to provide content such as music downloads to its online consumers, and finally the online consumer who wishes to buy that content and therefore use the micropayment system. In the BT *click&buy* arrangement, the consumer has an account and the value of the items purchased online in any month are added to the consumer's standard phone bill. It is a simple process but one which permits lower value Internet transactions for items where use of a credit card would be a barrier to the sale.

The micropayment provider will charge the music company a percentage fee on each transaction completed using the service. It will also probably charge an up-front integration fee for setting up the micropayment system and integrating it with the music company's website.

The service provider company, which we shall refer to as Micro, will confirm in the agreement that it will provide the micropayment service to the music company with the reasonable skill and care of a competent provider of such services.

In order to set up the service Micro will need to integrate its system with the website operated by the music business. The agreement will make clear that before the service is provided, a detailed process must be followed to establish and test the system integration between Micro and the music company.

In any event Micro will not offer any warranties that its system will be free from faults and the music company will be required to accept that failures of the service may occur from time to time.

Micro will usually state that there can be no guarantee of security on the Internet and therefore it will not warrant that it will be able to keep the music company's transactions secure.

It will be necessary for the micropayment service to be maintained at various intervals and Micro will make clear that for operational reasons it may change the technical specification of its service, or suspend it for maintenance or because of an emergency. In each case Micro will endeavour to give as much notice as possible to the music business.

The consumer who buys the music company's merchandise using the micropayment service will be billed per transaction and whatever the basis of that charge including value and when levied, that will be set out in the agreement between the music company and Micro. Any changes or additions to that basis must be managed by the music company as directed by Micro.

The whole payment process must be reported accurately and this will typically be done by Micro, providing the music company with information on a monthly basis in the form of a statement of account. This will detail the value of all online sales during the previous month, include an invoice from Micro to the music company showing Micro's charges, and any sales which Micro has been unable to collect from the consumer. Micro will withhold or recover monies paid to the music company if the consumer does not pay for the online items, or for example if the sum paid is duplicated in error. It may be that Micro will include a provision in its contract with the music company allowing it to charge a retainer on a percentage basis each month. This retention will cover anticipated non-payments by the music company's consumer and will be reviewed perhaps quarterly to ensure the retention is based on actual levels of non-payment over such period.

The agreement will place the obligation of security for passwords and usernames which the music company adopts for access to its website upon the music company itself. Micro may include a right to suspend its service if it believes that a breach of security has occurred.

No offensive or indecent material should be offered by the music company via its website by use of the micropayment system and Micro will reserve the right to terminate the service in such circumstances.

The intellectual property rights in the software which supports the micropayment service will be expressly reserved in favour of Micro or its licensors if in fact Micro has itself taken a licence of the software from a third-party provider.

The circumstances under which the agreement between Micro and the music company can be terminated will be set out, whether for reasons of breach, or if the commercial relationship is to come to an end for simple business operational reasons. In the event of termination Micro will call for the return of any material including hardware, software and documentation which it has provided to the music company in support of the service.

It can be seen that there are many issues to cover in a relationship between the music company and the micropayment service provider. Our review is illustrative but full legal advice must be sought if such a strategic relationship is being considered.

CHECKLIST

- Explore the various payment facilities now available for Internet sales. If likely to be providing products or services with modest prices, consider micropayment services.

- Examine the cost implications on entering into a micropayment facility with a provider.

CHAPTER 10

Agreements with Web Designers, Mobile Operators and Internet Service Providers

MUSIC WEBSITE DESIGN AND DEVELOPMENT AGREEMENT

A relationship which is vital to the online activity of a music business is that with its website designer. In the early years of e-commerce few businesses which elected to operate online gave much thought to the key terms they should have with their website designers. The industry was new and many website development firms had not grown from other businesses and thus on both sides of the arrangement, potential problems could not be appreciated.

As the industry matured and experience was gained on the part of those instructing website developers, problems began to be apparent. These tended to be issues around what happened when the website designer's services were to be dispensed with. There were disputes over ownership of intellectual property rights in the website, domain name transfer and hosting of the website.

Some ten years on most website developers work to standard contracts with their clients and the majority of clients now expect to sign such an agreement and are clearer as to what they wish to see in the contractual relationship.

For a music business there are some key issues to consider in the contract to be entered into with its website design and development company. In this section we will examine those matters from the perspective of the music business as opposed to the website design company. It is important to emphasize this as there are a number of issues where the designer and the music business will have different commercial expectations. It will often be a question of negotiation as to what forms the final contract. We will review those matters which the music business would find desirable.

The designer will be appointed on the basis of the terms and conditions in a 'music website design and development agreement' (the agreement).

The designer will be required to design the website in accordance with an agreed specification and in an agreed time period. This question of the specification is a frequent source of dispute. On occasion the music business may require certain functionality of the website but may not communicate its aims sufficiently to the website designer. The full functionality of the website must be clearly defined and the place to do this is in the technical specification. The specification usually forms a schedule to the agreement as this is the part which will change for each website produced by the designer whereas the contractual terms may well remain substantially the same from deal to deal.

The agreement will cover the fees which are to be paid by the music business for its website. It is not uncommon for those fees, once agreed, to be met over various intervals of the design process. For example, a certain percentage will be paid upon signing the agreement, further payments to be made upon presentation of the look and feel stage of the design, or at other testing phases, and the remaining sum a week after live running of the website once online.

Clearly the music business would want to retain as much control over the content of its website as possible and this impacts on the question of intellectual property rights. To enable the development of the website the music business will provide the designer with a good deal of material including text, photographs, video images, logos, trade names and so on. The intellectual property rights in those materials will almost certainly belong to the music business or a third party, such as the music artist or a record company. Therefore the intellectual property rights in that content will reside with the music business or be otherwise licensed to it by the third party. It will not belong to the website designer. The form of that intellectual property may be copyright in the text, photos or video, and perhaps trademarks in the name of the business or certain products or services it operates.

However, the website designer is being asked to design a website and the functionality of the website may well be the result of original work by the designer which in itself attracts copyright. Website designers will usually only grant a licence to their clients of their intellectual property but retain ownership themselves. This is because those rights represent the value to the designer in its enterprise. There are circumstances where the music business will want to expressly acquire the intellectual property rights in its website. If the contract between the two were silent on the point the designer would be deemed to own those rights as original author. Therefore if the music business does wish to hold the rights this must be made clear in the agreement. Typically the designer would charge a premium for the release of the rights to the music business.

The music business would wish to approve all content in its website before it goes live and this right should be stated in the agreement.

The music business in most instances will simply assume that the designer has appropriate personnel equal to the task of developing its website. However, it is a good idea to include a provision confirming that the designer will at all times have sufficient personnel to perform its contractual obligations under the agreement. It is common for staff in web design companies to move to other companies in the industry and often those staff are key in terms of their particular skills in certain aspects of web design. A music business could find itself facing a delay in construction of its website or, worse, the inability for certain desired features of the website to be capable of completion in the absence of appropriate personnel on the part of the designer. The agreement should include a clause giving the music business the right to terminate the agreement if this situation occurs.

As stated, most web design work is undertaken in stages and there are testing intervals which serve as useful opportunities to review progress and performance of the website designer. The agreement should contain provisions which allow the music business to terminate the contract if at those stages work is not satisfactory. However, the right to terminate would only arise following an agreed notification process to enable the designer to respond to any legitimate concerns the music business has over the construction process.

If the music business decides to make changes to its proposed website during the design process or after completion of the website then there should be a clear process to follow in the agreement. This issue is actually quite significant given the dynamic nature of website design and the competitive nature of the music industry. It is possible that a music business discovers an innovative service being offered by its competitor online, and wishes to make rapid changes to its own website to capture the new market. Any further costs associated with the changes requested by the music business would be notified to the music business first, under the terms of the change request procedure.

The period for which the agreement is to run must be stated. This can be for a fixed term, for example one year, and then run on a rolling basis until terminated by either party. This is more usual where the designer is to provide ongoing services to the music business such as consultancy support or training for the website. There must also be express provisions in the agreement dealing with the circumstances in which the agreement can be terminated early. This usually revolves around a significant breach by one of the parties of its obligations under the agreement. A standard clause would also see an ability to terminate if the other party becomes insolvent.

The consequences of termination must be made clear. If the website designer is in breach the music business will want to be able to recover material supplied to the designer which is central to the successful operation of the website. This might include all software documentation to enable a third-party designer appointed by the music business to load onto another server and ensure continuity of the music business's service.

There is always a need to maintain confidentiality with regard to each party's business. During the development phase and even thereafter, as long as there is commercial dialogue between the designer and music business, certain information will be revealed which is by its nature confidential. The music business may well be seeking to launch a new service to promote an artist which must be kept secret until the website is launched or that service promoted via the website.

In Chapter 7 we considered the Data Protection Act requirements. In the agreement it is important for the music business to ensure that the designer recognizes its obligations under the Data Protection Act if it is to store or process personal data acquired by it. The music business might seek an indemnity from the designer for unauthorized disclosure of such personal data which causes the music business to be in breach of the Data Protection Act and suffer financial penalty or loss.

It is often said that in litigation, there are no winners except the lawyers. Certainly the costs of going to court can be prohibitive and so even where there is dispute which cannot be resolved by discussion between the music business and the designer, actual court proceedings should be avoided where possible. One way is to enable an 'alternative dispute resolution' procedure to be included in the agreement. This is where both parties agree to appoint a mediator in the event of dispute in an attempt to reach agreement. It is a way to seek resolution without the costs of going to court. If the mediation cannot be concluded or if one party refuses to proceed on that route then the other party can still sue in the courts for redress.

CHECKLIST

- Always ensure a comprehensive website design and development agreement is signed with the website designer.

- Carefully consider who is to own the intellectual property rights in the website.

- Check how payment for the website is to be made and that there are no hidden extras such as content management charges for the designer updating the website.

- Make sure the circumstances for termination of the agreement are clear and what the consequences are for such termination.

- Include an alternative dispute resolution clause.

MUSIC WEBSITE HOSTING AGREEMENT

We have looked at the key features in the relationship between the music business and its website designer. The next vital marriage is that of the music business and the company which hosts its website. Website hosting services comprise the storage of a website and its content on a service provider owned or leased server.

Clearly the website operated by the music business must be capable of being supported continuously. It is likely that a range of services will be offered through it which each demand uninterrupted availability and access by the music fan. It is therefore of critical importance that the music business have in place an agreement with the provider of the hosting services which sets out clearly the service levels to be expected of the hosting company.

The following is a brief review of the issues to be covered in a website hosting agreement.

The music business will, despite the need for continuity, be asked to acknowledge that from time to time the hosting company's systems, servers and equipment will be inoperative or partly operational due to mechanical breakdown, maintenance, hardware or software upgrades or other causes beyond its control. In each case proper notification by the hosting company must be given to the music business. Occasional problems of this kind might be tolerated by the music business. However, repeated instances would be cause for termination of the relationship as discussed below.

The hosting company will probably include a clause stating that it will not warrant that the hosting services are fit for the particular purposes the music business may require.

The hosting company may seek to limit its total financial liability to the value of the hosting services provided in relation to the performance of its obligations under the contract. Moreover, it may exclude liability for consequential loss which the music business might suffer as a result of interruption to the hosting services. An example might be if the music business has a commercial relationship with a third-party company surrounding the music business website. If the website is not operational due to the hosting company's error, the financial consequences to the music business may not simply be its own losses, but also those of the third-party company who would look in the first instance to the music business for recovery of its losses. The music business must look carefully at the contract to see if it contains exclusions of this kind.

The hosting company will exclude liability for the content provided by the music business.

The agreement will make clear that it does not constitute any transfer of intellectual property rights which the music business has in the content it requires hosting.

The hosting company might want to use the music business logo or other reference to it in the hosting company's marketing of its own services. If this is the case then the agreement should state it clearly.

The hosting company should be asked to warrant that its services will be provided by appropriately qualified and experienced personnel using all reasonable skill and care.

The music business will be asked to confirm that it will install and maintain industry standard computer virus protection software and will take reasonable steps to ensure that any software it uses in conjunction with the hosting services will not damage or corrupt any system of the hosting company.

The music business will be solely responsible for dealing with any complaints about its content and music consumers will not be directed to the hosting company in the event of any such complaints.

Each party's right to terminate the contract will be set out. The music business will be required to meet the hosting charges and all other obligations imposed by the contract. If it fails to do so the hosting company will seek to terminate the contract. Likewise the music business should insist on very tight service-level obligations upon the hosting company and if these are breached by it then a right to terminate on the part of the music business should be included.

As is usual in any commercial agreement between businesses, if either party goes into liquidation or threatens to be wound up, such event will permit termination of the contract by the other party.

There will be an obligation on both the music business and the hosting company to maintain the confidentiality of the other's business information which has been revealed during the negotiation of the relationship and during the hosting arrangement.

As with all key commercial relationships between a music business and its strategic partners full legal advice should be obtained first. Remember whoever the music business deals with are themselves commercial entities and will seek to exclude or limit their own liability in the relationship as much as possible. In many cases it will be a question of bargaining power as to the coverage of such restrictions.

MOBILE COMMUNICATIONS SERVICE PROVIDER AGREEMENT

As the Internet and mobile apparatus develop, an increasing range of content is being offered online by the music industry. These include ringtones, polyphonic ringtones, logos, picture messages, Java games, screensavers and various other items such as competitions. These may use a combination of website downloads and SMS short codes with shared telephone short code numbers allocated to the music business by the provider of the service.

If a music business is considering providing such content it will usually need to find a partner company to provide the premium rate numbers, SMS short codes, managed content or interactive voice recognition services to enable the music business to offer the content to its telephone callers.

The relationship will require an agreement setting out the obligations and responsibilities of each party. We will now examine some of the provisions one might expect to find in such an agreement.

For ease of explanation we will call the provider of the service 'Provider'. It is important to appreciate that such arrangements are complex and typically the Provider will not be the operator of the telecommunications system itself. The Provider will have to contract with such a company for the provision or management of interconnection and that contract falls beyond the scope of this book.

The Provider will confirm that the services are not specifically designed for the music business and that the Provider is dependent on the telecommunications company and perhaps other third parties for the provision of the services. It will not therefore offer any assurances or guarantees.

The contract will continue usually until terminated by either party on notice in the case of termination for commercial reasons, or immediately if one party is in serious breach of its obligations. For example the Provider will terminate the contract if it receives a complaint or objection from the telecommunications company, the Regulator, the Government or other official body about the music business's services; similarly if the Provider believes that the music business is, or is poised to allow the services to be used for any unlawful purpose. The agreement may also be terminated if the music business does not adhere to any code of conduct published by the mobile network operators such as O2, T-Mobile, Orange, Virgin, Vodafone or '3'. The agreement would also terminate immediately if either party goes into liquidation or threatens to do so.

Another cause for termination on the part of the Provider is inadequate financial performance of the service operated by the music business, for example the usage of premium-rate numbers. Usually a minimum monthly figure must be achieved by the music business, for example £100 per month.

The Provider may terminate the agreement in the event of breach by the music business or it may restrict the service available to the business.

The music business will not have any ownership in the premium-rate numbers or SMS short codes. In fact the SMS short codes will be used by other customers of the Provider.

The Provider may reallocate numbers or codes where there are perhaps less than twenty calls per month to the premium-rate numbers or SMS short codes for three or more consecutive months, or for other reasons for termination as described above.

The Provider will seek to limit its liability in a variety of ways. It will state that it cannot guarantee a fault-free service or guarantee the capacity. It will not warrant that the equipment will be error-free or that the network will be continuous or fit for the purposes of the music business.

The Provider will periodically need to suspend the service for the purpose of system maintenance and will of course give the music business reasonable notice of such suspension.

It will suspend, restrict or bar the services if at any time the number of calls to the premium-rate numbers causes congestion or other disruption to the Provider's system. It can be seen that very clear dialogue must be had between the music business thinking of offering services to music fans via premium-rate numbers or SMS short codes, and the Provider. These discussions will include likely levels of traffic. It would be little use to the music business if its mobile phone campaign is so successful that it causes disruption to the Provider's system and is suspended, causing annoyance to the music consumer. Full discussion may reveal that the Provider may impose traffic restrictions on particular premium-rate numbers to preserve service quality. The music business will be required under the agreement to notify the Provider of any television or radio-based advertising campaigns or other promotions that are likely to result in sudden peaks in calls or SMS traffic so as not to risk failure of the system.

It may be that the service offered by the music business might require specific licensing or approval. The Provider will require that the music business obtains all necessary approvals, licences and permissions from any Regulator or other body and that such permissions remain in force.

The Provider will want the right to monitor all services and record any calls made to the premium-rate numbers or text sent to or from the SMS short codes used by the music business.

The music business will be required to supply to the Provider information and material from time to time requested, including advertising copy, promotional material and recorded messages which the Provider may use for billing and credit-checking purposes.

All advertising by the music business of the services it offers via the premium-rate and SMS short code service must be approved in advance in writing by the Provider.

The music business will have to confirm that its content does not infringe any intellectual property rights belonging to a third party and that the content is not defamatory, libellous or illegal.

The agreement will state that all advertising and promotional material used by the music business must comply with the relevant regulatory provisions relating to both the media within which the advert is placed and the content of the advert.

The music business will be required to have in place sufficient indemnity insurance in respect of the items it wishes to provide using the Provider's services.

The Provider will calculate its charges by reference to the data recorded or logged by it and not by the data recorded or logged by the music business. The Provider may provide the music business with a report or online statistics to give an indication of the traffic generated by the music business campaign.

The Provider will include provisions relating to clawback of monies overpaid to the music business. In fact the Provider will usually have the ability to include a retention, which is an amount to cover any actual or potential clawback.

The music business will be called upon to pay any fines levied by any regulatory body either upon the Provider or the music business itself. The Provider will impose an administration charge for having to deal with such issues. The agreement will also require the music business to hold harmless and indemnify the Provider against all liability which the music business incurs as a result of its service.

It may be seen that agreements of this kind cover a variety of issues and they are likely to favour the Provider of the premium-rate or SMS short code services. Clearly, the larger the music business and the scale of the campaign it is embarking upon may well dictate a more equal balance of responsibilities and liability in the agreement. If a music business is considering a launch of mobile services to its artists' fans to accompany its online activity, full legal advice must be obtained during the negotiation of the agreement.

CHECKLIST

- Ensure that the relationship between the music business and its website designer is properly set out in a website development agreement and includes precise terms covering intellectual property rights and any ongoing consultancy.

- Continuity of Internet service is vital to the music business and ensure that a detailed hosting agreement is entered into which sets out service-level guarantees on the part of the hosting company.

- If offering mobile services content ensure that a comprehensive agreement is in place between the provider of the premium-rate or SMS short code service and the music business.

CHAPTER 11

Strategic Agreements between the Internet Music Company and other Parties

As the music industry embraces new media, music businesses are seeking to leverage new platforms and are investing heavily in interactive development. The technology is evolving rapidly and in many instances the music business will not have the ability to develop new channels to market and offer the complete service to its target audience. Therefore it must enter into partner relationships with other companies that can support innovative formats and implement leading-edge technology. In this chapter we will consider some strategic commercial relationships which the music business might enter into in order to maximize revenue from its digital presence.

LINKING AND REVENUE SHARE AGREEMENT

The Internet is all about links. It is an established feature of websites to contain hyperlinks to other related websites and using broadband efficiency the visitor can seamlessly move from one site to another gathering a wealth of information. For websites offering a commercial service there is much to be gained by the monetizing of those relationships to other websites. As the convergence of technology and media advances with increased crossover of service and format, the music business might well explore strategic relations with other parties providing different but complementary services.

In the music industry there is increased crossover both of platforms and service delivery. A record company can offer material promoting its artists which would include CDs, DVDs, music downloads and certain merchandise. However, with branding of artists being such a vital part of the marketing of bands it may be that the record company needs to source development of related digital products from other software disciplines. If those related products are offered online by their manufacturer or developer there could be commercial merit in the record company entering into a strategic relationship to secure revenue from sales of the product which are attributable to a link from the record company website to the developer website.

If a music company is to establish formal links with another commercial entity it is important to embody the commercial basis of that relationship in a linking and revenue share agreement. In addition, there are a number of legal considerations which should also form the content of that agreement.

In this section we will take as an example an online relationship between a music company website and a video games website. We have assumed that the record company will take a commission percentage on all sales of the video games achieved via the link from the record company website.

Typically the record company R will agree to set up, with the assistance of the video games company V, a connection with R's software to V's website. This link will provide a seamless connection and enable R's artist fan base to connect to perhaps the order section or shopping basket of V's website.

The agreement will confirm that both R and V will be entitled to refer to each other as 'alliance partners' or a similar description to highlight their commercial connection in all their advertising and marketing material.

In our example we have envisaged that R will receive commission on sales of V's games. The agreement will therefore deal with this arrangement and specify the commission rate. It will state that V will have the sole right and responsibility for processing all orders made by R's consumer fan base. R will acknowledge that all contracts for the sale of the games to those fans are between V and the fans, and not R and the consumers.

It might be that V is free to set the price of the games although possibly in such a key relationship there could be some agreement between R and V over pricing. Either way the actual pricing model needs to be set down in the agreement.

V will be under an obligation to identify customers originating from R's website and log them as 'R and V customers' or an appropriate designation to reflect their nature.

V will also be required to supply a monthly statement of all such transactions. The statement would need to show clearly all sales, refunds or deferred sales during that month. The statement would set out full details of the revenue achieved, the gross profit generated and of course the commission payable to R.

V would likely commit to paying R following receipt of an invoice from R, which invoice might be rendered on the first day of the calendar month for the previous calendar month. There would be an express exclusion of liability for V to make a payment to R in cases where full payment has not been made by an 'R and V customer' or where a refund has been given by V in relation to the same. The usual payment terms might apply, for example 30 days from receipt of R's invoice.

An agreement of this kind by its nature would doubtless be for a limited period. The pace of development of new technology means that products are superseded quickly. The term of the agreement therefore needs to be made clear: it might be for a fixed term of two years. The agreement must be capable of being brought to an end sooner in certain specified circumstances by either party. An obvious termination trigger would be if either R or V is in material breach of an obligation under the agreement. If R or V enter into liquidation of threatened liquidation or some other form of insolvency-related arrangement, termination needs to be immediate. The agreement would state that all commission payments due to the date of termination must be met by V.

The matter of intellectual property is very important to both the media and software development industries. With the increased convergence of the two examined elsewhere in this book it is important to set clear the ownership rights of the various intellectual property elements which combine to perfect the relationship between R and V. Both R and V will retain all right, title and interest in their names, logos, trademarks, service marks, copyrights and proprietary technology. The agreement will provide for the granting of a revocable, non-exclusive, worldwide licence to use, reproduce and transmit their respective names, trademarks and proprietary software on their respective websites solely for the purpose of creating the links between the websites.

The agreement will also on the matter of intellectual property rights state that neither R or V shall copy, distribute, modify, reverse engineer or create derivative works from the other's works. For example, V will not do this as regards the musical content provided by R, and R will not seek to develop its own version of V's online games.

Each will offer an indemnity to the other that they have not infringed the intellectual property of any third party in the creation of their respective works;

further, that they are not in violation of any applicable law or regulation. This issue is important – the Internet's global reach can mean that certain products would not be lawful to make available in certain countries. It might be that the content of certain musical works would be offensive to a particular region or jurisdiction. The same might be true of the video game. There could be issues of libel in both the music and the game content. Other commercial considerations where an indemnity should govern include misleading advertisement laws (see Chapter 12) or unfair competition laws. Given that both parties are operating their strategic relationship using Internet technology, there would be an indemnity for computer viruses and other destructive programs.

It is possible that as R and V seek to promote their joint arrangement, they make statements about each other's product to other commercial or media organizations. The precise ambit of what they each might say in relation to the promotion of the product would be dealt with under the terms of a joint marketing agreement rather than this linking agreement. However, in this agreement there would be an indemnity against all liability, losses, damage and professional fees brought by a third party, arising out of a breach or a representation made by either R or V about the music or the games.

V might seek to restrict its total financial exposure to R for any breach R is responsible for, to the total amount of commission paid by V to R in the calendar year of the date of the legal claim.

There would be a need to maintain confidentiality in relation to any information imparted or made available to the other as a result of the commercial relationship. This would be amplified in the linking agreement. 'Confidential information' would be defined to include all non-public information concerning the business, technology and structures of the disclosing party. The receiving party would agree to keep the same in confidence and not permit any employee, agent or other person working under its direction to disclose or disseminate the information. Reasonable steps must be taken to secure confidential information by both R and V where storage is provided by electronic means which will almost certainly be the case.

Neither R or V will be able to assign (transfer) the benefit of the linking agreement to any third party without the prior consent of the other party.

Finally, the agreement will be expressed to be governed by English Law.

An agreement of this kind will contain many more specific commercial terms agreed as between a record company and video games company based on the actual deal struck. However, the above review sets out some principal provisions a music business should address if considering a strategic Internet linking deal with another party.

MUSIC SOFTWARE LICENCE

We have considered the position which governs the sale of merchandise from a music business website. However, there is increased pressure upon record companies and the industry as a whole to fight the threat of technology with technology. This means developing new products or devising new marketing initiatives which offer the consumer fan more than the simple music CD or even music download. It is possible that some form of Internet-based technology application could be offered to fans via a download. This might be software which enables an enhanced experience for the consumer interested in a particular artist. If that offer is a software application then the only way it can be safely made available to the user is by licensing it. In other words, the music business would retain its proprietary rights over the software but grants the consumer a limited right to access and use the software.

The risk with any Internet-based system is that the moment a new service is launched online it can be adopted around the world. Therefore if the music business as content provider cannot manage an international rollout within a period of weeks, someone else could steal the market opportunity that has been created. The question then arises of how the music business can achieve legal protection for its web-based system. The answer is in what is known as a 'web-wrap' software licence. The web-wrap software licence has been devised to satisfy the needs of technology and mass marketing over the Internet. The licence is to be used where it is almost impossible to obtain the signature of the end user to a licence before software is delivered unless an electronic signature is used. The next best thing is constructive acceptance of the licence terms.

As we noted in our review of contract formation online, the terms and conditions of the web-wrap licence must appear on screen either at the ordering stage and/or before the software can be downloaded to ensure its full content can be read and accepted by the proposed end user.

The following are examples of typical provisions a music business might wish to include in its licence of Internet software. Clearly, the precise terms of such a licence will be heavily influenced by the nature of the actual product being licensed and what it is designed to offer. Nonetheless our review serves as a helpful guide.

At the opening of the licence agreement one should include a statement advising the user that before they click on the 'I Accept' button at the end of the document and download the software they must carefully read the terms and conditions of the licence agreement. Further, by clicking on the 'I Accept' button and downloading the software they are consenting to be bound by and becoming the licensee to the licence. They should be told that if they do not agree to all of the terms of the licence they should click the 'I Do Not Accept' button and not download the software.

The agreement would then confirm that when the user clicks the 'I Accept' button the music business grants them a non-exclusive, non-transferable licence for the software product including any electronic documentation (the 'software'). Typically the licence would allow the user to use the software on a single computer system and will prevent it being transferred electronically from one computer to another or used over a network. Many young Internet users and teenage music fans are adept at finding ways to copy software and they routinely visit friends' homes and thus use a variety of computers. The licence will state that the software is not free or shareware and there is a licence fee.

Upon accepting the licence the consumer will be asked to undertake not to copy the software or disassemble, decompile or reverse engineer the software. Nor must they translate, lease, modify, redistribute or sub-license the software or create derivative works.

The music company would want to be free to create new versions of the software or upgrades. It would state that whilst it has no obligation to notify existing licensees of those upgrades, the same will be made available at the same Internet website from which the licensee downloaded the software. The cost of the upgrade would of course be stated as well.

It is important to impose a restriction requiring the end user to agree not to display the software on a public bulletin board or the World Wide Web or Internet chat room or by any other unauthorized means. In addition, the end user must be prohibited from using the software for any immoral, illegal or harmful manner which would include the creation of any computer virus, Trojan horse or other destructive computer program.

It is highly likely that the music company will have either developed the software in-house or otherwise engaged the services of an external software developer. In either case the company may well have reserved the intellectual property rights in the product. However, if the product were, as is common, licensed from another company, perhaps the software developer, then clearly the music company would not own the intellectual property rights itself. On the basis that the music company does have title to the intellectual property then it would wish to retain those rights in the licence agreement it is granting to its online end user. It would reserve all copyright, trademarks and other intellectual property rights subsisting in or used on connection with the software. These would include all images, animations, audio and other identifiable material relating to the software.

The licence agreement must deal with the question of termination both at the instance of the music company, and its online consumer. The licence agreement would state that the end user may terminate the licence at any time by destroying the software and any documentation and state that no licence fee is refundable. The agreement should state that the music company may terminate the licence agreement at any time if the end user is found to be in breach of any of the terms.

ONLINE LICENCE BETWEEN LABEL AND ARTIST

This book examines the legal considerations which affect those associated with the music industry when using the Internet commercially. The form and extent of such use will vary of course, with most record companies still producing physical CD products distributed to retail outlets in much the same way as they have done for decades. They will have websites but these are restricted to the offer of merchandise, artist news and possibly sample music facilities. This model is unlikely to be replaced wholly by the Internet. However, there are an increasing number of record companies established solely for music promotion and distribution via the Internet. Then there are the legitimate online music provider websites who simply make available music catalogues against payment.

At the time of writing, the EU is considering the introduction of an online copyright licence. The creators of online music services such as composers, lyricists and performers would be able to secure a single pan-European copyright licence. The proposal by the European Commission is designed to boost the growth of legitimate online content services in the EU and close the gap with the US in webcasting and streaming. The main aim is to ensure that more royalties are distributed to right holders across national borders.

The agreement we will examine next is intended to cover the arrangement by which a record company wishes to use the recordings of an artist on its website and sell those recordings via the website. The scenario envisages an online record business offering to promote and make available to the public musical works posted to it by bands and solo artists. The website will, as we have seen in Chapter 3, require full legal terms and conditions which the record-buying website visitor will need to click through before completing the purchase. The following review is of the terms of the licence which will govern the relationship between the record label and their artist for the provision of the songs to the label.

The artist thus agrees to licence certain musical content to the label for exploitation via the Internet. The artist will grant the label the non-exclusive right for an agreed period of time to exploit the musical content throughout a specified territory via the Internet. This right will also permit the label to make any alterations to the content technically required to make the music available to the user via the medium. Combined with this right will be a right typically for the label to use any promotional material from the music. Further, the label will want to retain data relating to the artist on a database and deal with such data for the purpose of marketing the content. The label will gain ownership of the database it builds up of contacts to whom the artist's music is distributed.

The online music company will want the ability in its sole discretion to choose not to exploit the music or any promotional material if in its reasonable opinion it is necessary for legal, technical or marketing reasons. It might also attempt to include a provision which states that if the artist is unable to make their music available to the public due to the act or default of the label for a specified period (for example, 30 days), then the only remedy open to the artist would be termination of the online licence by notice in writing.

The issue of royalties of course is fundamental to music distribution. Typically the Internet licence will make clear that all royalty payments due to the artist will be automatically processed in accordance with the licensing terms of the music alliance (see Chapter 5) provided the artist registers the recorded work with the recognized royalty collection agency or publisher. The label will then deduct and retain the royalty from the gross revenues achieved by the sale of the music via the website. The matter of royalty rates music publishers and composers charge for music downloads is the subject of some unease at the time of writing. The British recording industry has joined forces with online music services to challenge the royalty rate for digital downloads. The British Phonographic Industry (BPI) and seven online companies – AOL, Apple iTunes, MusicNet, Napster, RealNetworks, Sony Connect and Yahoo – have pursued the Mechanical Copyright Protection Society and the Performing Rights Society in the Copyright Tribunal. The MCPS-PRS alliance wants to charge a higher royalty rate for songs downloaded from the Internet than for those on CDs. Publishing royalties on CDs currently comprise 6.5 per cent of the retail price. The alliance wanted to charge a 12 per cent rate for most online music services but as a concession suggested a temporary rate of 8 per cent while the online industry is still under development. The BPI assert that the music alliance's tariffs threaten to harm the development of the legal online and mobile music markets. They claim that the advent of a new music format does not warrant an increase in royalties. The MCPS-PRS alliance contend that the proliferation of music means artists get a small slice of an even smaller pie. In fact the BPI and the music alliance have been negotiating the download royalty rate for years, but the matter has become more pressing in the last year or so as the popularity of digital downloads has soared.

There are other commercial terms which one would expect to see included in the online music licence between label and artist just as they would appear in more traditional agreements. Thus, the label would commit to the provision of accounts to the artist within a specified period of time perhaps twice a year. The accounts would cover the preceding period and be accompanied by the appropriate payment due to the artist.

The music company will want to obtain certain warranties from the artist in relation to the music which they agree to make available:

- first, usually the company would want the artist to warrant that they are free to enter into the agreement and have attained the age of 18;

- second, that the artist has not entered into any arrangement which might conflict with the licence to be granted and is under no restriction or prohibition which might prevent the artist from performing any of their obligations under the licence.

The online music business can do its best to mitigate its exposure by the imposition of such a warranty.

The music company should add a provision requiring that the performances rendered by the artist shall be first-class technically and artistically.

Another warranty required would be that the services rendered by the artist be original and shall not under the laws in force in any part of the world be obscene, blasphemous or defamatory of any person, or infringe any right of copyright, right of privacy, performers' rights or indeed any other right of a third party. It will be recalled elsewhere in this book that it is not possible however to exclude liability for defamation. In addition, the artist shall render the services to the best of their skill and ability in a professional and workmanlike manner in full cooperation with the label and all people engaged by the label.

The company would also need to have absolute discretion on the issue of promotion and advertising and all other related matters.

Another desirable clause the company should include in its licence agreement is an indemnity by the artist. This would be an agreement to indemnify fully the company against all claims and any associated costs arising as a result of any breach by the artist or non performance of any of the artists warranties and obligations under the licence agreement.

The label would impose an obligation of confidentiality on the artist in terms of confidential information gathered by virtue of entering into the licence agreement.

The details of exactly which musical works are to be licensed to the record company for online distribution would usually be set out in a schedule to the licence agreement.

The licence agreement outlined above can be offered on the music website itself with the artist agreeing to its terms by clicking through the terms as discussed elsewhere. In any event, under the provisions of the E-commerce Regulations 2002 the full terms of the licence must be capable of being printed off in hard copy.

ONLINE MUSIC MAGAZINE SUBSCRIPTION AGREEMENT

Record companies use their artist websites to offer an array of content which is exclusive to their artists' Internet fan base. This is in part to attract more users to the website on a regular basis and retain their loyalty and also because the very nature of the medium permits the provision of dynamic content which cannot be made available in any other way. Much of this material is offered free and other merchandise or advance concert information is offered for sale albeit at special rates for early confirmation. Another source of revenue for the website is the production of an online magazine or journal containing the latest news or in-depth interviews with the artist together with other content of direct interest to the fan. This might be offered free but can also be delivered via the website on a paid-for model. Online journals offer a means of monetizing the website audience by providing further advertising and sponsorship opportunities.

As described earlier, in 2005 the artist Robbie Williams launched an online subscription service transforming him into a retailer and cashing in on intellectual property ranging from images to live footage and interviews. The website is thus a full commercial business rather than a marketing strategy. Subscribers have access to a library of over 1000 images and exclusive behind-the-scenes video clips together with every Robbie Williams video.

In this section we will review some of the items which a provider of an online music journal might include in the legal terms which would be posted on the website. A common example of the use of this online bulletin is by a record company to its artist fan base. However, online journals might be offered by other commercial providers connected with the music industry or indeed by the artist themselves. Whoever makes available the magazine, the same considerations will apply and the guidance provided in this section should thus be read accordingly. Once again it is important to remember that in so doing the provider is asking the website visitor to enter into a legally binding contract and, as we have seen, a contract must contain a number of conditions for it to fulfil the legal criteria in English law and also to safeguard the interests of the content provider. In common with the previous commentary in this book on strategic legal agreements, since it is envisaged that the online magazine will be targeted at a consumer audience and more than likely a young audience, there are significant consumer law protections which must be adhered to by the provider. These laws govern any contract with consumers and not merely those conducted online.

The following review is prepared on the assumption that the magazine will be subscribed on a single-user licence; that is, offered to say individual fans to be accessed by them against their personal password. However, multi-user or corporate-wide licences can be prepared but these require additional provisions not dealt with in this work. The subscriber would need to be pushed through the legal terms and conditions when they first register their details to subscribe for the journal in the manner of a click-wrap contract. Thus the website must be designed in such a way as to make sure that the legal terms must be clicked through before the subscription application can be completed. Likewise the requirements of the E-commerce Regulations 2002 apply (see Chapter 4).

First, it is vital to ensure that the subscriber has legal capacity to enter into the contract and must therefore be over the age of 18 to subscribe or require parental authority to sign up for the magazine.

The music business will be offering a non-exclusive, non-transferable licence to use the subscription service. Usually that licence will permit the display by the visitor of the material electronically on a single computer or download or print one copy of the journal.

It is important to build in some protection in terms of restricting the use of the material. So, for example, clear statements confirming that the user cannot store, download, transmit, copy or reproduce the content must be incorporated. The user must not be allowed to sub-license, lease or assign the rights in the content to any other person. They should be prevented from making the content journal available on a network or allowing anyone else to use the content other than in accordance with the licence terms and conditions now being put before them.

The need to specify that the online journal is for their private non-commercial use is clear. If the music business established that any of the above limitations on use have been breached by the user then the company must have the ability to terminate or suspend access to the magazine.

As the subscriber is being asked to pay for the journal, full information on how payment is to be made must be included. The price needs to be fixed for the date and time of the order and needless to say it is incumbent upon the music business to ensure that prices are maintained accurately and if the subscription price increases, the latest detail is posted to the website.

As considered elsewhere remember that the music website is not an offer for sale of any content or products available by accessing it. Thus, the proper approach is to make clear in the subscription terms that the music business is entitled to refuse any subscription request placed by the fan. An electronic confirmation must be sent to the user only when the subscription request is in fact accepted by the company. Now, suppose the user signs up to receive the magazine. Is it possible for them to cancel their order under the provisions of the Distance Selling Regulations 2000? (see Chapter 8). The answer is no. An online magazine contract is not subject to the seven-day cancellation right. It is certainly open to the music business to elect to offer a cancellation option within a prescribed timescale but that would be simply a matter of commercial gesture rather than a legal obligation.

Then we come to the matter of collecting the personal information about the subscriber. This is likely to consist of their full name, address, email address, telephone number and almost certainly, their age and gender. Such data is of course a valuable resource to the music business. However, the precise use to which the personal details might be put by the company must be made clear. As the Internet enables highly targeted and real-time information to be delivered, a record company for example might wish to offer different versions of the content according to age and gender to their artist fans. The personal information thus given will allow sophisticated marketing strategies of this kind and the online questionnaire will probably be far more detailed to obtain a precise user profile. It should be the responsibility of the subscriber to give accurate information.

The issue of personal profile also arises on geographical considerations. Major record labels are global concerns but even more modest labels may have correspondent relations with other labels in other countries. It might be that the label wishes to offer specific content to users in particular countries based perhaps on an understanding of the buying behaviour previously displayed by those users or for very cogent legal reasons. In any event the question of whether to accept subscribers only from the UK or from other countries via the website needs to be addressed. The better view is to restrict access to UK subscribers only, and if it is intended to offer variation to the content to non-UK residents then those visitors should be directed via alternative arrangements.

The music business must therefore state that they have used their best endeavours to ensure that the content complies with English law but make no representations that the service is appropriate to locations outside the UK. A statement to the effect that if the magazine or any products made available in it infringe any applicable law in another country then the user is not authorized to view the magazine and must exit immediately.

A clause stating that English law will govern the contract is essential.

The journal may well feature further web links to other websites referred to in the text of a particular story about a band or artist. It is important to include an exclusion clause that the music business makes no representations about any other websites which the subscriber might access through the journal; further, that those other websites are not necessarily endorsed by the music business, and that no liability for financial loss or any other damage will be accepted by the company if the user suffers the same by virtue of acting on information or viewing the content of those other sites. As we have discussed elsewhere however, this exclusion will work in the context of certain possible areas of harm, such as someone suffering poor service or non-supply of merchandise from that other website. It will not, though, shut out any liability on the music business for defamatory or offensive material displayed on that other website. Thus, the obligation on the company to constantly monitor the content of websites linked to their site is significant.

As with any Internet service there are many things which can disrupt access to the network and over which the music business has little control. Therefore make clear that the subscription service cannot be guaranteed continuously or without interruption and liability cannot be accepted for periods of downtime. Obviously there are questions of reasonableness here. The user is paying for a service delivered over the Internet and they have reasonable expectation that they will be able to access the same at times of their choosing. If the service were to suffer repeated interference then a user would be well within their rights to demand cancellation and return of their subscription fee. No exclusion clause will protect a music business in such cases.

Certainly one would wish to include exclusions for financial loss which might be suffered by a subscriber's indirect or consequential loss or damage, or loss of data, profit or business alleged to have been suffered by the user. The music business would also want to make clear it will not be responsible for computer viruses or infections which the user claims were contracted via the website. The subscriber must be made aware that it is their own responsibility to ensure that their computer system meets necessary technical specifications both to use the service, and to view it with the benefit of anti-virus and other security check software.

CHAPTER 12

Advertising Music and Merchandise Online

In this chapter we will consider the controls which exist in the UK on the use of advertising via the Internet and mobile telephones.

A music company's advertising on the Internet will be interactive and based on a model in which the customer comes to it. Until the advent of the Internet, interactive advertising or marketing activity has been conducted face to face. The World Wide Web enables music businesses to engage their consumers in the advertising itself.

A major challenge to music advertisers over the next decade will be finding ways to fully utilize this capability. Involving the online consumer in the advertising message can build long-term customer commitment.

Still the most common form of Internet advertising is *banner* advertising. Banner adverts are no longer just static files. They may include animation, direct response and other interactivity. Web advertising is fairly simple in concept. The company decides it wants to place a banner advertisement on a website. It negotiates with the owner of the website. Usually, advertising rates are based on a certain cost per thousand impressions (CPM).

These impressions are measured by the owner of the website based on the number of times the banner is seen by visitors. At the end of the period, the website owner invoices the advertiser. It is calculated by multiplying the CPM by the number of impressions during that period.

Before considering online advertising, it is well to briefly set out the legal background to advertising production in the UK. In this country, advertising is regulated by voluntary codes. There are also many statutes which affect advertising.

BRITISH CODE OF ADVERTISING, SALES PROMOTION AND DIRECT MARKETING

The British Code of Advertising, Sales Promotion and Direct Marketing is now in its eleventh edition and came into force on 4 March 2003. It replaces all previous editions.

This is the principal voluntary code in the UK. It is drawn up by the Committee of Advertising Practice.

The Advertising Standards Authority (ASA) is charged with the duty of monitoring compliance with the code. The ASA is independent.

The code applies to traditional media such as advertisements in newspapers, magazines and mailings but it also covers emails, text transmissions and other electronic material. In addition the code governs advertisements in non-broadcast electronic media including online advertisements in paid-for space, for example, banner and pop-up advertisements.

Therefore a music business wishing to embark on an advertising campaign using email, text messaging or the Internet must abide by the provisions of the code.

We will now examine the principal terms of the code as they apply to an online music business. It is important to appreciate that the ambit of the code is wide and it does not simply apply to advertisements in the traditional sense. The code contains various definitions. For example products which fall within its domain encompass goods, services, ideas, opportunities, prizes or gifts; promotions are also covered. Thus, a music business wishing to offer via its website a prize to win artist merchandise, or running an online opportunity to claim a CD gift must comply with the code.

There are some general rules which apply to an online, email or text promotion or advertisement for music goods or services. These include:

- All marketing communications should be legal, decent, honest and truthful.

- All marketing communications should be prepared with a sense of responsibility to consumers and to society.

- All marketing communications should respect the principles of fair competition generally accepted in business.

TESTIMONIALS

There are many other requirements; for example concerning testimonials and endorsements. A music business should hold signed and dated proof, including a contact address for any testimonial it uses. Unless they are genuine opinions taken from a published source, testimonials should be used only with the written permission of those giving them.

The testimonial must relate to the music product being advertised.

Testimonials alone do not constitute substantiation and the opinions expressed in them must be supported, where necessary, with independent evidence of their accuracy.

Fictitious testimonials should not be presented as though they are genuine.

There are clear guidelines on the protection of privacy of people the music business might wish to associate with the online or mobile advertisement. If referring to people with a public profile, for example a music artist, references that accurately reflect the contents of books, articles or films may be acceptable without permission.

Prior permission may not be needed when the marketing communication contains nothing that is inconsistent with the position or views of the person featured.

However, in implying any personal approval of the advertised product, the online music business should recognize that those who do not wish to be associated with the product may have a legal claim.

PRICING

Any Internet, mobile content or text advertising must ensure that stated prices should be clear and should relate to the product advertised. The music business must ensure that prices match the products illustrated in for example the photograph in the advert.

All prices quoted in marketing communications addressed to the public should include VAT and other non-optional taxes and duties imposed on all buyers.

A recommended retail price (RRP) or similar, used as a basis of comparison should be genuine; it should not differ significantly from the price at which the product is generally sold. Concert DVDs for example offered via the website of the music business at a discount from the RRP in shops must be a genuine reduction.

AVAILABILITY OF MERCHANDISE OR SERVICES

The music business must make it clear if stocks are limited. Products must not be advertised unless marketeers can demonstrate that they have reasonable grounds for believing that it can satisfy demand. If the merchandise becomes unavailable, the music business will be required to show evidence of stock monitoring, communications with outlets and swift withdrawal of marketing communications whenever possible.

Merchandise which cannot be supplied should not normally be advertised as a way of assessing potential demand unless it is clear that this is the purpose of the marketing communication.

The music business must not use the technique of switch selling, where its sales staff criticize the advertised merchandise or suggest that it is not available and recommend the purchase of a more expensive alternative. They should not place obstacles in the way of purchasing the merchandise or delivering it promptly.

GUARANTEES

If the online music business is offering a guarantee it will be legally binding on it. The word 'guarantee' should not be used in a way that could cause confusion about consumers' legal rights. Any substantial limitations on the guarantee should be spelled out in the marketing communication. Before commitment, the online consumer should be able to obtain the full terms of the guarantee from the music business. This of course once again brings into question the use of sending mobile broadcast advertisements which may have limitations on screen size or size of content transmitted. In such cases clear reference to the music business website and the legal terms and conditions which appear on the website must be made.

If it is a money-back guarantee, the music business must provide a cash refund or cheque promptly to those claiming redress under the offer.

Remember it is necessary for the music business to ensure its target users recognize it is a marketing communication. The email message or mobile broadcast should be designed and presented in such a way that it is clear they are marketing communications. Unsolicited email marketing communications should be clearly identifiable as marketing communications without the need to open them.

ONLINE SALES PROMOTIONS

As stated above, the code also applies to sales promotions and regulates the nature and administration of promotional marketing techniques. Those techniques usually involve providing a range of direct or indirect additional benefits, usually on a temporary basis, designed to make merchandise or services more attractive to purchasers.

The music business must conduct any promotion online or by mobile equitably, promptly and efficiently and should be seen to deal fairly and honourably with consumers. They should avoid causing unnecessary disappointment.

The music business wishing to promote merchandise or services should be able to demonstrate that it has made a reasonable estimate of likely response and that it was capable of meeting that response.

Using phrases such as 'subject to availability' do not relieve promoters of the obligation to take all reasonable steps to avoid disappointing online participants.

The business should not encourage consumers to make a purchase or series of purchases as a precondition to applying for promotional items if the number of those items is limited.

If the business is unable to supply demand for a promotional offer because of an unexpectedly high response or some other anticipated factor outside its control, it should offer refunds or substitute products.

The online or mobile promotion should be conducted under proper supervision and adequate resources should be made available to administer them. The music business should allow adequate time for each phase of the promotion, distributing the goods, collecting wrappers and the like and announcing results. It is important to bear in mind that online and mobile promotions are capable of immediate response by consumers and that is their appeal to both music business and fan. However, that means the business must be able to fulfil with similar speed.

A free offer may be conditional on the purchase of other items. Consumers' liability for costs should be made clear in all material featuring the offer. An offer should be described as free only if consumers pay no more than:

- the minimum, unavoidable cost of responding to the promotion, for example the current public rates of postage, the cost of telephoning up to and including the national rate or the minimum, unavoidable cost of sending an email or SMS text message;

- the true cost of delivery.

The music business should not charge for packing, handling or administration.

Essential conditions for an online promotion

An online promotion should specify clearly before any purchase (or before, or at the time of entry or application) the following detail if no purchase is required:

- how to participate, including significant conditions and costs, and any other major factors reasonably likely to influence consumers' decisions or understanding about the promotion;

- the start date and the closing date if applicable for purchases and submissions of entries or claims. Prize promotions and promotions addressed to or targeted at children always need a closing date.

If there are any geographical restrictions which apply, this should be stated. If there are any other restrictions such as personal ones (for example, age), technological restrictions, or conditions of availability (for example, email response, not text message), this should be stated. The music business should state any need to obtain permission to enter from an adult or employer.

SENDING ELECTRONIC MARKETING MESSAGES TO CHILDREN

Special care of course needs to be taken when music promotions are addressed to children (people under 16) or when products intended for adults fall into the hands of children. Given that many music artists have a large following of fans under 16 it is particularly important that the music business understands its obligations when sending electronic promotional messages.

The way in which children perceive and react to marketing communications is influenced by their age, experience and the context in which the message is delivered. So, marketing communications which are acceptable for young teenagers will not necessarily be acceptable for young children. The music business therefore needs to take that into account.

Marketing communications addressed to, targeted at or featuring children should not exploit their credulity, loyalty, vulnerability or lack of experience. They should not be made to feel unpopular or inferior for not buying the advertised product. They should not be made to feel that they are lacking in loyalty if they do not buy or do not encourage others to buy a particular product.

The advertisement should be made easy for them to judge the size, characteristics and performance of any product advertised and to distinguish between real-life situations and fantasy.

Adult permission should be obtained before they are committed to purchasing complex and costly products.

Promotions addressed to or targeted at children should not encourage excessive purchases in order to participate and among other things should contain a prominent closing date.

PENALTIES FOR BREACHING THE CODE

There is a much stricter regime relative to advertising regulations in contrast to the general law. A music business's advertisement claims require a level of justification in excess of that necessary for its editorial.

There are penalties for breaching the code.

If an online advertisement breaches the code, the ASA will ask a music business to withdraw or amend its advertisement. Other sanctions include adverse publicity, the refusal of further space, removal of trade incentives and finally legal proceedings.

These sanctions are by referrals from the ASA to the Office of Fair Trading (OFT) under the Control of Misleading Advertisements Regulations 1988 (CMAR). The OFT can obtain an injunction against a company to prevent it from repeating the same or similar claims in future advertisements.

The first problem which Internet advertising highlights is the proper application of advertising standards in the right circumstances. The distinction between advertising material and editorial on a website can become blurred.

This is exacerbated by the seamless linking of pages on the web, which renders it difficult to separate the two. This difficulty may lead to the inadvertent extension of advertising content restrictions to editorial content.

At the time of writing, there is no reported case concerning how an English court would approach the question. The issue was considered in the Irish case of *Dunnes Stores Limited* v *Mandate*:

> *The case was founded on the Irish equivalent to the UK Control of Misleading Advertising Regulations 1988. A trade union representing a claimant's workforce placed an advertisement in the national press seeking to justify strike action by the union's members over Christmas pay. The Irish Supreme Court held that the trade union's advertisement had nothing to do with the promotion of the supply of goods or services and so was not 'advertising'.*

When considering advertising and the Internet, the most vexing issue is jurisdiction. The difficulty in properly regulating electronic commerce advertising is trying to apply national frameworks of laws and regulations to adverts disseminated to the world at large.

An online advertisement is, in theory, subject to the laws of every country in which it is accessed by an Internet user. Thus far the ASA have focused on websites which originate in the UK. If it is faced with a foreign website, it may be able to refer the complaint to an equivalent regulatory body in the foreign jurisdiction.

The breach of non-domestic regulations as a result of the global reach of the Internet was illustrated in *United States* v *Thoms*, a US court case.

> *In that case, the operators of a pornographic electronic bulletin board in California were convicted of criminal obscenity laws by a federal court in Tennessee. The conviction was founded on Tennessee standards of decency.*

At present there is no international unanimity on the issue of which country's law applies to Internet advertising. The approach which seems to be adopted is that the laws of the country of 'publication' will apply; that is, the country in which there is evidence of 'directed' activity. This is illustrated by an incident involving the English-registered Virgin Atlantic Airways:

> *In 1996 Virgin was fined by the US Department of Transportation for a misleading advertisement on its UK server. The inaccuracy related to the quoting of erroneous fares and listing a fare that was no longer available on flights from the USA.*

The simple inclusion of information on the music business's website will not, of itself, be conclusive evidence of directed activity if there is something about the information making it clear it is targeted at customers in a particular country.

The language of an advertisement may be relevant to an extent. A disclaimer contained on the website may help to clarify who is included in the target audience. An example might be 'this offer is only available for consumers in France'. Such a disclaimer will however be construed narrowly and have no legal effect in some countries.

Whilst it will be impractical to obtain legal clearance in every jurisdiction throughout the world, there are some general principles to adopt:

- Obtain legal and trademark clearance in each target country and in countries in which the music business has a presence or assets.

- On a purely practical level, the business might consider how costly it might be to change its online advertisement if it were challenged.

- Would a competitor in fact be able to prove actual damage? Finally, it may well be that the authorities in a given country will take a laissez-faire approach to an Internet advertisement.

If the music business engages the services of an advertising agency, the issue of the music business's Internet advertising strategy must be discussed fully with the agency.

The risks that a business could incur liability for breach of foreign advertising regulations makes it essential for the contract with the agency to lay down clear lines of responsibility for ensuring legal compliance of advertising materials.

INTERNET MUSIC ADVERTISING AGREEMENT

In 2005 there was a huge increase in the acquisition of Internet companies by larger media groups predicated on the strong growth in Internet advertising, which the previous year amounted to $10 billion. Growth prospects for Internet advertising are forecast to be 20 per cent in 2006. This compares to traditional media activities, particularly newspapers, which are recording single digit advertising revenue increases. The business world is now recognizing that Internet advertising is no longer a fantasy but an integral part of media businesses.

A significant development of the commercialization of the Internet has been the commercial sponsorship of websites.

Website marketing and advertising is highly important to a successful e-commerce strategy – one only has to reflect on the plethora or television advertisements which promote corporate and retail websites. Usually such promotion is part of a wider advertising campaign.

An organization may wish to sell to others rights to advertise on its website. This advertising can be in the form of banner adverts, hyperlinks and browser windows which start automatically. It may wish to distinguish between a sponsor, who is entitled to a more prominent place on the site, and other advertisers who will receive lesser billing.

From the point of view of the advertiser, it will want to be clear not only about the rights it receives in isolation but also its position within the hierarchy of rights.

If a music business is entering into an arrangement with another company to enable that company to advertise on its website, the Internet advertising agreement should cover the following:

- **Rights** The rights being granted in respect of a website should be determined. Is the advertiser to have exclusive rights? Are there categories of advertising within which the advertiser will have exclusivity? For example will it be the only video games developer on the site?

- **Payment structure and triggers** It should be considered whether payment will be calculated on a base fee, per display, click-through or on ultimate sale.

- **The responsibilities of the advertiser** in relation to appropriateness of adverts should be clearly understood.

- **Licences** It would be prudent to enter into limited licence for the use of graphics and/or text and trademarks used in the advertisements.

- **Inclusion of indemnities** to limit liability should be considered.

- **Termination of the agreement** should be clear. In addition, the agreement should set out what will happen upon termination. Usually, materials should be destroyed and web pages changed. If the agreement is terminated at short notice, all payments due under the same should become immediately due and payable.

- **Nature of relationship between the advertiser and music business** The agreement will only be for advertising cooperation. It should state clearly that it does not create an agency or joint venture between the parties.

- **Positioning and size** An advertiser will wish to specify where on the website its advertisement will appear. The form and size of the advert relative to other text and other graphics should be clear. With paper-based advertising campaigns, sizes are constant. However, Internet advertising involves the consideration of the working of hypertext mark-up language and the operation of the web browsers which will be used to access the sites. An advertiser may wish to set up the technical details of how, in particular, its logo is created so as to ensure that it both downloads at an acceptable speed and is attractive.

- **Updating** Some advertisers may want some contractual assurance that the web page itself will be changed over time to keep up with new versions or releases of relevant browsers, and conversely, that it will remain usable with older versions.

- **Website promotion obligations**   If a site relates to a campaign by a company in other media, advertisers may wish to have assurances about the promotion of the site within that campaign, such as by the inclusion of the website URL (Uniform Resource Locator) on posters and other forms of advertising. Conversely, and particularly where there is one major sponsor, the music business might wish to oblige that sponsor to promote the site as part of the sponsor's own advertising.

- **Hypertext links**   Both the music business and the advertiser will have concerns relating to the hypertext links from the advertisement to the advertiser's own web page. Advertisers will want to make sure that the link is correctly created and the site owner is obliged to update it correctly if there is a change in the URL of the advertiser's website. The advertiser may also wish to ensure that the link can be triggered either from the text message or a graphic. The music business should ensure that the link to the advertiser's website will not give rise to any liability to third parties for defamation.

- **Intellectual property**   Advertisers will wish to specify the extent of the right of the music business to use any trade or service marks on the site and to ensure that it applies the marks consistently with any standard guidelines. The form of the advertising in general may concern the advertiser and they will wish to have prior approval of relevant copy. The music business should seek an indemnity in respect of third-party claims arising from use of the advertisers marks on the Internet.

- **Information about visitors to the site**   Who visits the site will be of interest to the advertiser and the music business. This is because the music business will need to justify their advertising rate card. and the advertiser will need to judge whether the music company's webpages are an appropriate place to advertise.

RULES RELATING TO MUSIC RINGTONE SALES

It is worth a brief review of recent rules which, although targeted at the mobile phone operators, have relevance to a music business given the increased convergence of services provided by music service providers and the mobile service providers. In Chapter 2 we considered the potential problems when contracting with children and teenagers. As a result of concern expressed about the manner in which mobile phone ringtones are made available, recent changes have been introduced by the mobile telephone operators. The safeguards were because of the Crazy Frog ringtone discussed earlier. The mobile operators recognize that there is a need for effective controls that help consumers from becoming victims of misleading advertising and which set out clearly what is expected of content providers. O2, 3, Orange, T-Mobile and Vodafone have introduced the safeguards at network level. The new rules include the following:

- A standard message which includes details of service charges and billing frequency must be prominently displayed within any form of advertising for a subscription text services. In the case of television advertising, this new standard message must be permanent and static for the full duration of the advert and be accompanied by a voiceover.

- A mobile phone user joining a subscription text service must be sent a free reply text message from the content provider confirming the user's subscription commitment. The service operator must also provide a standard or free-rate customer helpline number and include this number in the reply text message.

- All mobile phone users joining a subscription text service must be sent a notification text message either monthly or when £20 has been spent on that service, whichever comes first. The text must remind the user how to unsubscribe.

- All service operators must operate a website which includes terms and conditions for the service.

These new safeguards are in addition to the existing consumer protection rules contained in the Independent Committee for the Supervision of Standards of Telephone Information Service's (ICSTIS) Code of Practice. In addition they build on the common STOP command introduced recently by the mobile phone industry to enable customers to cancel subscription services by texting the word 'STOP' to the text short code related to their service. The STOP command will now be extended to cover any form of text, WAP or media messaging-based marketing to enable consumers to stop the receipt of any marketing messages.

ICSTIS has also introduced a prior-permission requirement for open-ended services that cost users more than £20 in total. Permission will only be granted if service providers demonstrate that their services and advertising material meet certain standards designed to prevent consumer confusion and harm.

TELEVISION WITHOUT FRONTIERS DIRECTIVE

The Television Without Frontiers Directive (89/552/EEC) was adopted on 3 October 1989 by the European Council and amended on 30 June 1997 by the European Parliament and the Council Directive 97/36/EC. The Directive established the legal framework for the free movement of television broadcasting services in the EU to promote the development of a European market in broadcasting and related activities such as television advertising. So if a broadcaster is licensed in one member state, they are free to broadcast in another country in the EU without the need for further licensing. It was designed to avoid the prospect of multiple regulations because there would only be one country of origin.

The Directive is now the subject of a second revision. The reason is that it has very quickly become out of date with the rapid development of technology in the last few years. Communication technology has transformed the way in which broadcast transmissions can be accessed and in particular the Internet opens up new vistas for content distribution. In an age when television can be delivered to a mobile phone the European Commission decided to launch a review of the original Directive to accommodate new technology.

The reason why it is useful to consider the proposals here is because of the convergence of broadcast media and the increase in web-based movie transmission of music content. It is no longer necessary to employ complex and expensive equipment to broadcast to a wide audience and if a music business is considering advertising or promotion via web-based television services then it must understand the direction the law is heading.

There are immediate problems the regulators need to consider. For example, the traditional broadcast model sees content delivered at predetermined time schedules via standard television sets. In effect, the programmes are 'pushed' to the viewer. However, with Internet broadcasts the position is more complex: first, the content is available for access at the time of choosing of the user and thus the programmes are 'pulled' by the viewer when they want them; second, there is far more variation in terms of what constitutes a programme with regard to what can be sent via the Internet. The new rules being considered only cover commercial broadcasts but the regulators appear to be making the distinction between services controlled by the broadcast operator – linear services – and those where the consumer chooses – non-linear services. It is likely that detailed controls in terms of advertising will probably only apply to linear services and not therefore a high degree of content which is delivered over the Internet.

Further difficulties arise in drawing the line between linear and non-linear services with an increasingly sophisticated array of delivery mechanisms. There are going to be a range of hybrid services where visual content is delivered using a combination of routes to the consumer.

The new Directive is therefore no longer just concerned with television; it really spans all audio-visual content including of course music video broadcasts. A new Directive is envisaged by 2007 requiring implementation in all EU member states by 2010.

There are some reservations about the practical effect of the new Directive. Content regulated in Europe would not have any impact on the vast majority of content providers who operate outside the EU. The rules may not work effectively for music audio-visual websites hosted overseas, which of course can be viewed in Europe. In addition if regulation of Internet broadcasts is introduced in Europe, there is a danger of a handover of commercial and legal advantage to content providers based elsewhere in the world.

CHECKLIST

- Ensure the music business understands its obligations under the Advertising Standards Authority Code and that the code applies to Internet-based promotions.

- Pay particular attention to the rules for advertising to children.

- Consider the rules relating to music ringtone sales.

CHAPTER 13

Electronic Signatures and Online Music Sales

As we noted in Chapter 2 it is possible to form a legally binding contract by simple exchange of email. The parties would usually accept that the individuals who sent the messages were who they purported to be and that they have necessary authority to enter into the contract. However, as online business has developed there are higher value deals being struck and these should not in any view be conducted on the basis of email correspondence. They should be concluded based on properly drafted legal agreements reflecting the nature of the deal. If for example the music business were to require those whom it wished to agree terms with to sign a contract online the question arises of how this can be achieved. The real objective in having someone sign a document is to bind them or their organization to the terms of the agreement. In the physical world one can see the person or even verify their signature on a fax document. It is reasonable not to assume that the signature is forged.

With the Internet it is more difficult to guarantee the authenticity of the person with whom a contract is to be concluded. For this reason in recent years electronic signatures have developed which provide that authenticity. Conducting business using electronic signatures requires a different mindset from conventional contract management because there are different risks.

In this chapter we will examine how the identity of a party to an online commercial contract can be authenticated using electronic signatures. It is fair to say that at the time of writing electronic signatures have not been widely adopted by industry at large. The market for such devices has not yet developed. However, they exist and can be utilized, and so a brief review is warranted.

As we have seen with much of the law examined in this book, it is the EU which dominates the legal regime to which online business is subject. In December 1999 the European Commission adopted the Electronic Signatures Directive as a response to the development of legislation by each member state.

The main thrust of the legislation is twofold: first, it imposes a requirement on each member state to provide for the legal recognition of electronic signatures; second, it provides mutual recognition.

Before we examine the new legal framework which governs electronic signatures, it is helpful to view it in its proper full legal context.

FORGERY

To what do we refer when we talk of forgery? Forgery of one's signature is a risk, albeit modest, which all of us face in everyday life and in business.

The forgery is usually done as a prior step to the commission of some other crime, most often a crime of deception, which will result in some material advantage (most obviously gaining money or other property) to the forger.

In the UK under English law, forgery and counterfeiting are regulated by the Forgery and Counterfeiting Act 1981.

A person is guilty of forgery if they make a 'false instrument' and for this purpose 'instrument' is defined by Section 8 of the Act:

> ... 'instrument' means that
>
> (a)...any document, whether of a formal or informal character;
>
> (b)...any disk, tape, soundtrack or other device on or in which information is recorded or stored by mechanical, electronic or other means.

It can be seen that the Internet can constitute an instrument for the purposes of the statutory definition. Section 9 of the Act states:

> (i) an instrument is false for the purpose of this part of this Act:
>
> > (a) if it purports to have been made in the form in which it is made by a person who did not in fact make it in that form; or

(b) if it purports to have been made in the form in which it is on the authority of a person who did not in fact authorize its making in that form; or

(c) if it purports to have been made in the terms in which it is made by the person who did not in fact make it in those terms; or

(d) if it purports to have made in the terms in which it is made on the authority who did not in fact authorize its making in those terms;

or

...

(h) if it purports to have been made or altered by an existing person but he did not in fact exist.

(ii) a person is to be treated...as making a false instrument if he alters an instrument so as to make it false in any respect...

FORM OF AN ELECTRONIC SIGNATURE

The term 'electronic signature' actually covers many forms of electronic technology: it can even be a retinal scan to verify personal identity. As will be seen in this section the law recognizes the rapid pace of development and has attempted to legislate the use of electronic signatures in a technology-neutral fashion. In other words, it does not simply assume one form of electronic signature for the purpose of drafting laws which will govern for many years to come.

For present purposes we will refer to the most commonly understood and thus far utilized form of electronic signature in industry. In effect the electronic signature is a stamp which appears as an icon and which can be attached to an electronic document. Its appearance and application is straightforward; its underlying technology is not. It relies on cryptography.

Cryptography is a method of sending the contents of a message in code, used from ancient times to the present. In the context of the Internet, cryptography is the science of keeping communications private. Cryptography has long been applied by banks and is an essential tool for electronic commerce.

Cryptography can be used as the basis of an electronic signature or to keep electronic data confidential. It also ensures that the integrity of such information is preserved. A central element of cryptography is encryption – the transformation of data into an unintelligible form. Encryption is the process by which a message is disguised sufficiently to hide the substance of the content. It involves turning normal text into a series of letters and/or numbers which can only be deciphered by someone who has the correct password or key. Encryption is used to prevent others reading confidential, private or commercial data, for example an email sent over the Internet.

In essence, contemporary cryptographic systems change readable symbols into a second set of unreadable symbols using a mathematical process controlled by a number. This number is called a key.

The following shows the process:

Music business A writes to record company B 'We agree your terms'

The message is encrypted as '196421043520418N620181727227'

To read the message, record company B must know how the message was encrypted. If they know the key to the unintelligible symbols, they can work out the message when they receive it. This example does not demonstrate the use of a mathematical formula, but is intended to illustrate how the concept works. There are two types of mathematical families that permit the message to be disguised.

Encryption technology therefore provides the ability to create and validate electronic signatures through the use of what is called 'asynchronous' or 'public key' cryptography. The system uses two keys, one to encrypt and one to decrypt a message. It is this feature that is used for signatures.

By use of this process a document can be signed using one's private key. Anyone can then use the corresponding public key to verify the identity of the signatory as only their private key will correspond. However, that process of itself cannot identify and verify the owner or holder of the private key. To do that a trusted third-party arrangement is necessary.

CERTIFICATION AUTHORITIES

Certification authorities or trusted third parties are public or private bodies that certify the connection between a person and their public key. The certification authority guarantees the authenticity of the public key.

Put simply, the trusted third party certifies that to the best of its knowledge the identity of the signature holder is that which is claimed. The certification authority issues an 'electronic authentication certificate' which has the following characteristics:

- it identifies the certification authority;
- it identifies the subscriber;
- it contains the subscriber's public key;
- it is digitally signed with the certification authority's private key.

The electronic authentication certificate also contains other information, such as the level of enquiry carried out by the certification authority before issuing the certificate.

It is necessary for the music business to provide the certification authority with a copy of the public key number and proof of identify, together with sufficient credentials to demonstrate an authority to deal with high value transactions. When music business A sends a message to record company B, it also sends record company B a copy of its certificate. Record company B's computer will decrypt the message according to the key they have been given.

At the same time, the certification authority will confirm to record company B that:

- music business A is who it is purports to be;
- the certificate has not been revoked nor has expired.

In summary, the role of certification authorities is to provide certificates that establish the identity of the owner of the public key.

ELECTRONIC COMMUNICATIONS ACT 2000

In 2000 the UK Government introduced the Electronic Communications Act. The main purpose of the Act is to help build confidence in electronic commerce and its underlying technology.

The Act was in fact the first piece of UK legislation written specifically for the Internet. It provides an approval scheme for businesses and other organizations providing cryptography services, such as electronic signature services and confidentiality services. Second, it gives legal recognition of electronic signatures and third it removes obstacles in other legislation to the use of electronic communications and storage in place of paper.

The Act is in three parts of which the first two have relevance to this book.

PART I – CRYPTOGRAPHY SERVICE PROVIDERS

This part concerns the arrangements for registering providers of cryptography support services, such as electronic signature services and confidentiality services. The Act creates a register of approved providers. Section I places a duty on the Secretary of State to establish and maintain a register of approved providers of cryptography support services, and specifies what information is contained in the register. The public have right of access to the register and any changes to it must be publicized.

The idea behind the register is that it will be voluntary but will promote minimum standards of quality and service to be met in relation to cryptography support services. The Government has indicated that if the self-regulatory scheme works, there will be no need to set up a statutory scheme.

The provisions in the Act relating to the establishment of the statutory scheme are subject to a 'sunset clause'. This states that if a statutory scheme has not been set up within five years then the Government's power to set one up will lapse.

Cryptography support services include:

- confidentiality – securing that such electronic communications or data can be accessed or put into an intelligible form; that is, restored to the condition which it was before any encryption or similar process was applied to it, only by certain persons;

- authenticity – ensuring, by use of an electronic signature, that the authenticity or integrity of electronic communications or data is capable of being ascertained;

- registration and certification – in relation to certificates, time stamping of certificates or documents, key generation and management, key storage and providing directories of certificates.

The Act makes clear that the approval scheme for cryptography support services only includes those services primarily which involve a continuing relationship between the supplier of the service and a customer.

PART II – FACILITATION OF ELECTRONIC COMMERCE

This part of the Act makes provision for the legal recognition of electronic signatures. It will also facilitate the use of electronic communications or electronic storage of information as an alternative to traditional means of communication or storage.

Perhaps the most obvious change the Act makes is that it provides for the admissibility of electronic signatures and related certificates in legal proceedings; that is, in court.

Section 7(2) Electronic Communications Act 2000 defines 'digital signatures' as:

Anything in electronic form as...is incorporated into or otherwise logically associated with any electronic communication or electronic data and purports to be so incorporated or associated for the purpose of being used in establishing the authenticity of the communication as data in the integrity of the communication or data, or both.

The courts will decide on this question of authentication or integrity of a message in the event of dispute.

In addition it is possible for a music business to contract with another business on how their respective electronic signatures are to be treated.

An electronic signature can be used as evidence of authenticity or integrity in court proceedings. Section 7(1) allows an electronic signature or its certification to be admissible as evidence on this question.

There are three elements to establishing authenticity of an electronic communication:

- whether the communication or data comes from a particular person or other source;

- whether it is accurately timed and dated;

- whether it is intended to have legal effect.

One concern raised during the Government's consultation period highlights this issue. The outdated definitions of words such as 'writing' and 'signature' in law were significant barriers to the development of electronic commerce in this country.

The Act includes a power in clause 8 to enable ministers to draw up secondary legislation to permit such requirements to be met electronically. For example, the Department of Trade and Industry used powers under the Act to amend the Companies Act 1985 to enable companies to communicate with shareholders electronically. Large music businesses can now send out notifications to shareholders of meetings and other matters required under the Companies Act by email rather than post. When there are thousands of shareholders, that is a useful ability.

PART III – MISCELLANEOUS AND SUPPLEMENTAL

This part of the legislation is concerned with the modification of telecommunication licenses including territorial extent of the Act.

CHECKLIST

- An electronic signature has the same legal effect as a physical signature.

- Ensure the music business understands how electronic signatures operate with the use of certification authorities.

CHAPTER 14

Disability Discrimination Issues for Music Websites

DISABILITY DISCRIMINATION ACT 1995 AND WEB ACCESSIBILITY BEST PRACTICE

It is important to appreciate that the Disability Discrimination Act 1995 has been in force for over ten years. When it was introduced it did not contemplate the Internet and specifically websites as within its ambit. At that time whilst those in the new media sector were well aware of the Internet and its commercial potential, legislators were not.

In essence the Act makes it unlawful for a service provider to discriminate against a disabled person by refusing to provide any service which it provides to members of the public. A service provider would include a web development company and most likely a music website operator.

In 2004 the Disability Rights Commission in the UK launched an investigation into 1000 websites of which over 80 per cent were next to impossible for disabled people to use. They warned firms they could face legal action under the Disability Discrimination Act.

However, in most cases where a website is found to be in breach, usually the Disability Rights Commission would warn the site operator first rather than simply go ahead and sue. Therefore legal action would probably not be pursued as the site would be corrected following the warning.

The World Wide Web Consortium (W3C) is the Internet standard-setting body. It is widely believed that if a case comes before the courts, the W3C accessibility guidelines will be used to assess a website's accessibility and decide the outcome of the case.

The W3C offers levels of compliance. Priority 1 guidelines, which must be satisfied according to the W3C, and Priority 2, which should be satisfied and are the EU recommended level of compliance.

In 2004 the Disability Rights Commission prepared a report based on their investigation of websites. The report is not law but it is a useful guide to the kind of problems faced by disabled or impaired people as regards websites. At the time of writing there are no reported legal cases on breach of accessibility.

The impairment groups represented in the user testing for the report were:

- blind people who use screen readers with synthetic speech or Braille output;

- partially sighted people who may use screen magnification;

- people who are profoundly deaf and hard of hearing;

- people with specific learning difficulties such as dyslexia;

- physically impaired people whose use of the web may be affected by their lack of control of arms and hands, by tremor and by lack of dexterity in hands and fingers.

The report makes a number of recommendations to improve the position and these include:

- Websites commissioners should formulate written policies for meeting the needs of disabled people. This might include ensuring that disabled people with a range of sensory, cognitive and mobility impairments are involved from early on in the process of website design and development.

- Those who provide and oversee education and training of web developers, including those who sell web-authoring tools, should promote an understanding that good practice entails attending and responding to the needs of disabled people. This might include ensuring that training modules covering these needs form an integral part of any continuing professional development or product support.

- Web designers themselves should accept that good practice entails attending and responding to the needs of disabled people. This would involve taking steps to familiarize themselves with how disabled people use the web and with their needs in web accessibility.

- The Government should raise awareness, for example by publicity campaigns aimed at web designers and commissioners.

- Web designers should involve disabled people in the design and testing of websites at an early stage.

- Web designers should not rely exclusively on automated accessibility training.

- Developers of automated accessibility checking tools should enhance their functionality to make them more useful to website commissioners and website developers.

- The designers and providers of assistive technology should enable and encourage users to keep their products up to date.

It is helpful to consider the key problems experienced by impairment groups according to the Disability Rights Commission report findings. Such a review will assist the music business in properly developing its website to ensure the website meets Disability Guidelines. The report did not concentrate on music websites but rather websites across a range of activities.

Blind users

- Incompatibility between screen-reading software and web pages, for example the assistive technology not detecting some links or it proving impossible to highlight text using text to speech software.

- Incorrect or non-existent labelling of links, form elements and frames.

- Cluttered and complex page structures.

- ALT tags on images non-existent or unhelpful. (An ALT tag is a text description that is displayed when the cursor is moved over an image.)

- Confusing and disorienting navigation mechanisms.

Partially sighted users

- Inappropriate use of colours and poor contrast between content and background.

- Incompatibility between accessibility software, for example for magnification, and web pages.

- Unclear and confusing layout of pages.

- Graphics and text too small.

- Confusing and disorienting navigation mechanisms.

Physically impaired users

- Confusing and disorienting navigation mechanisms.

- Unclear and confusing layout of pages.

- Graphics and text size too small.

- Inappropriate use of colours and poor contrast between content and background.

Hearing impaired users

- Unclear and confusing layout of pages.

- Confusing and disorienting navigation mechanisms.

- Lack of alternative media for audio-based information and complex terms/language.

- Inappropriate use of colours and poor contrast between content and background.

- Graphics and text too small.

Dyslexic users

- Unclear and confusing layout of pages.

- Confusing and disorienting navigation mechanisms.

- Inappropriate use of colours and poor contrast between content and background.

- Graphics and text too small.

- Complicated language and terminology.

There any other pointers for the music business to adopt best practice in its website. These include:

- Provide a text equivalent for every non-text element.

- Ensure foreground and background colour combinations provide sufficient contrast when viewed by someone having colour deficits or when viewed on a black and white screen.

- Until user agents allow users to freeze moving content, avoid movement in pages.

- Divide large blocks of information into more manageable groups where natural and appropriate.

- Clearly identify the target of each link.

- Use the clearest and simplest language appropriate for a site's content.

CHAPTER 15

Whose Law Applies to Internet Music Sales?

It is easy to overlook the obvious fact that the Internet is a global medium which means that a website is available for view from anywhere in the world. In many instances the music business may not really be targeting their merchandise or services at jurisdictions across the globe. They might wish to limit their online activity to the UK only. A number of websites operated by record companies are tailored for a given geographical territory. However it is also common for music websites to make available merchandise or services to international visitors to the site. At first view it might not appear obvious why we have to consider questions of legal jurisdiction in the context of online music distribution. As will be seen, it is however vital for any music company contemplating commercial Internet activity to appreciate the impact jurisdiction will have on its business.

A contract formed online has the potential to produce transnational disputes between the parties. We have seen in Chapter 3 that a music business would usually state in its website terms and conditions that English law will govern its online contract. Whilst this is a vital inclusion there are certain instances when supplying merchandise or services via the Internet from the EU where strict rules must be followed.

It is important for a music business to understand with certainty where it can be sued and where it can take legal action. When we refer to the question 'Whose law applies to Internet music sales?' we are really considering two issues: first, the jurisdiction or country in which a dispute will be heard; and second, whose set of laws will apply to that dispute, regardless of where the trial is held. The English courts are required to follow certain rules on jurisdiction and choice of law. This is the issue to be examined in this chapter.

BRUSSELS REGULATION 2001

On 1 March 2002 the Brussels Regulation on Jurisdiction and the Enforcement on Judgements in Civil and Commercial Matters (2001 OJ L012,16.01.2001) was introduced. The Regulation replaced the former Brussels Convention. It is necessary to first establish if the Regulation applies.

We will consider first the question of the proper jurisdiction. This issue relates to which country the music business website operator can be sued in and indeed take legal action.

A vital issue is where the defendant to a commercial dispute is domiciled. This is because under the Brussels Regulation someone domiciled in an EU member state can be sued in the courts of that state. So for example, if a UK music business finds that the copyright in its website is being infringed by a German company, the UK business can sue the infringer in the German courts. This concept of domicile also applies to contracts formed over the Internet. Clearly, if a music business were to sue a company for copyright infringement or indeed any other matter, the defendant would either be domiciled in a member state or a non-member state. If the domicile lies within a member state the Brussels Regulation rules will apply. If the defendant is domiciled outside a member state (anywhere else in the world), other legal rules prevail.

It is necessary to make a distinction between an individual who is domiciled in a country and a company so domiciled.

INDIVIDUAL DOMICILE

In the case of an individual that person is deemed domiciled within the UK only if they are resident in the UK and it can be shown that the individual has a substantial connection with the UK. That will depend on the nature and circumstances of their residence. However there is a presumption that being resident for the last three months or more will constitute this 'substantial connection'.

If an individual is not deemed to be domiciled in the UK for the purposes of the Brussels Regulation, it is necessary to then establish if the individual is domiciled within another EU state. If that person is not regarded as being domiciled within the EU, then the Brussels Regulation will have no bearing on the commercial dispute.

There is a simple test which must be applied to establish if an individual is in fact domiciled in another EU member state. The test is if the other state would regard the individual as domiciled there. The Brussels Regulation prescribes that the persons domiciled must be assessed from the particular state's legal perspective.

If the individual is not domiciled in any EU member state, the test is two-fold: first, the individual must be resident in that non-EU country; second, the nature and circumstances of residence must indicate that the individual has a substantial connection with that country.

CORPORATE DOMICILE

The Brussels Regulation makes clear that a company or other legal person is to be regarded as domiciled in the state where it has its statutory seat, central administration or principal place of business.

To establish whether a company is domiciled in the UK the test to apply is as follows. If the company or other legal person was incorporated or formed under a law which is part of the UK, and its registered office or other official address is in the UK, or if its central administration or principal place of business is in the UK, then UK domicile will be established.

A frequently asked question in the context of Internet-related disputes is whether a company which is based in the UK can avoid the jurisdiction of the English courts simply by using a server offshore? The answer is that it cannot. The ownership, control or access to a website in the world is irrelevant to the principle of jurisdiction under the Brussels Regulation.

Having established that a company or other legal person is not domiciled in the UK for the purpose of the Brussels Regulation, it is necessary to settle whether domicile lies in another EU member state. The Brussels Regulation will not apply to a commercial dispute if the company or organization is not domiciled within the EU.

Once again there are two tests to establish if a company or organization is domiciled in the EU though not in the UK.

In the first instance the English courts must be satisfied that the company or other legal person was formed or incorporated under the law of that other EU member state. Alternatively, that its central management and control is exercised in that EU state. The corporate entity must not have been formed under the law of any part of the UK or shown to be regarded by the courts of the EU country to have its seat within an EU state.

If these various tests do not establish that the defendant in a commercial dispute is domiciled either in the UK or another EU member state, then the Brussels Regulation will not apply.

Once it has been determined where the defendant is domiciled the defendant in a commercial dispute may be sued in the courts of their or its domicile or in the courts for the place of performance of the obligation in question. The are certain exceptions to this rules which are not relevant for our purposes but one exception which does relate is if the contract has a specific jurisdiction clause.

SALE OF GOODS OR SUPPLY OF SERVICES CONTRACTS

Where goods are sold or services supplied, unless it has been agreed otherwise, there are two presumptions applied as to the place of performance of those contracts. So for example where music merchandise is sold over the Internet to a consumer, the relevant court is the member state where the merchandise was delivered or should have been delivered. The same approach applies to contracts for the supply of services, that is, the relevant court is the one in the EU country where the services were provided, or should have been provided. If these presumptions do not apply, it is necessary to establish where a place of performance of the obligation was.

The most important point to stress is that if a music business operates a website from within the EU it is vital to include a jurisdiction clause in the online contract if the principal obligations are to be performed outside the home state of the music business.

ARTICLE 15 (1) BRUSSELS REGULATION

It is important to note that all EU-based consumers can sue and can only be sued in their home state. Thus, a UK-based music business operating online may find itself being drawn into litigation away from the UK. This would be a problem not least because the music business would have to instruct a UK lawyer who in turn would need to instruct a lawyer qualified in the particular jurisdiction. Whilst some international law firms may have offices based in that jurisdiction the professional fees of such transnational dispute can be considerable.

One might think that the issue of proper jurisdiction when dealing with consumers is straightforward. Certainly it is clear enough that the Brussels Regulation provides protection to consumers in relation to consumer contracts.

Article 15 (1) of the Regulation defines a 'consumer contract' thus. It is one which can be regarded as being outside the consumer's trade or profession where the contract is:

(a) for the sale of goods on instalment credit terms or;

(b) a loan repayment by instalments, or for any other form of credit made to finance the sale of goods or;

(c) in all other cases, the contract has been concluded by the person who pursues commercial or professional activities in the member state of the consumer's domicile, or by any means, directs such activities to that member state or the several states including that member state and the contracts falls within the scope of such activities.

It is this category of contract at Article 15 (1) (c) above which causes difficulties with Internet activities. There are two situations where activity might be 'directed' to a member state and hence invoke the protection in favour of the consumer of the Brussels Regulation.

First, the Regulation will apply it where the Internet music business pursues its commercial activities in the consumer's member state and the contract falls within the scope of such activities. For example, the activity of the music business might be to sell music CDs to consumers in France. If the contract at issue involved the online sales of such CDs to French consumers the Regulation will apply.

The second scenario where the Brussels Regulation will apply is where the music business by any means directs its commercial activities to the member state of the consumer domicile, or to several states including that member state and the contract falls within the scope of such activities. This is a complex area of law and needs to be examined in more detail.

If the online music business pursues commercial activity in the consumer's member state the position is as follows.

Here, the contract being sued upon must fall within the scope of the activities being pursued in the member state of the consumer's domicile. However, the Brussels Regulation has an additional requirement: this pursuit of the activity within the consumer's member state must also relate to the consumer's contract under dispute. It is not enough for a music company for example to target its activities at a particular EU member state of the consumer's residence or at a number of member states which included that member state. The contract must also be concluded within the framework of its activities. It is necessary therefore for a music business to consider all of its activities within each particular member state of concern. It will be necessary for the music company to be certain that any contracts it enters into with EU consumers in that member's state are not related to any other commercial or professional activities pursued in those member states.

Article 15 (1) (c) becomes even more difficult in its application when one considers a second situation of its application. This is where the supplier 'by any means' directs commercial professional activities to the member state of the consumers domicile. When considering this Article in the context of Internet activity, whether the Internet is accessed by the consumer via PC or mobile apparatus, the question is 'When is a website "directed" to a member state?'

The courts will be required to decide on this test on a case-by-case basis. However, it is clear that an Internet site simply being accessible is not sufficient for Article 15 to be applicable. A factor which will be relevant is if the website solicits the conclusion of distance contracts (see Chapter 8) and that a contract has actually been concluded at a distance. In such circumstances it is possible to argue that the music website is being directed towards particular consumers in the EU.

One issue to note is that the language or monetary currency which the music business website uses is not relevant for the purpose of the test of 'directing activity'.

It is thus the actual conduct of the music business in the particular member state that determines whether or not activities are in fact directed to that member state.

It is helpful to consider some examples to illustrate the operation of the Brussels Regulation. If an Italian consumer cannot transact with a German classical record label website, but nonetheless still views it, it is clear that the German label's commercial activity will not be held to be directed at Italy. This would be the position even if the website was presented in Italian.

In the UK, the Department of Trade and Industry have confirmed that to establish whether a website falls within Article 15 (i) (c) it is necessary to look at the nature of that website.

The UK approach is based on the following. The simple fact that a transaction can take place via the website in, for example, France, does not mean that the website has been directed at France. The determining factor is the 'nature' of the website. It can be seen that this issue is susceptible to controversy and it is likely to give rise to disputes on applicability of the Brussels Regulation to a particular business activity of a music business offered online.

The importance of Internet terms and conditions on a music business website is clearly paramount. It would also be wise for a music business, for example based in the UK, to specify on its website a menu of EU countries which are specifically excluded from its online activity. In addition the technical formatting of the website itself may permit the shielding of consumers from a particular country, although this, of itself may not guarantee suitable exclusion.

CHOICE OF LAW

We have considered above the question of the proper legal jurisdiction and the effect of the Brussels Regulation. That issue related to which country the music website operator can be sued and take legal action.

The next issue to consider is the actual choice of law. For example will it be English law, French law, a particular US state law? It is inevitable that the Internet will permit ever more contracts to be formed between parties from a variety of legal jurisdictions.

ROME CONVENTION

The Rome Convention permits a choice of law which can govern a contract. The Convention applies throughout the EU but in the UK, it is incorporated into the Contracts (Applicable Law) Act 1990. The Convention applies to all contracts made after 1 April 1991.

There are two forms of contract which can be made over the Internet for the purpose of the Rome Convention:

- where the contract actually specifies the law that will govern the contract and this is agreed;

- where the law that will govern the contract between the parties has not been agreed.

Any UK commercial activity conducted over the Internet should, as a matter of course, include an applicable law clause in the Internet terms and conditions (see Chapter 3).

The Rome Convention makes clear that a choice of law can be express, as in the case where the website terms and conditions make it clear those laws will govern the online contract. It should be noted that a choice of law can be express even though it is not actually specified in the contract. It may instead be demonstrated by the terms of the contract or the particular circumstances of the case. Therefore, an express choice of law may be deemed to have been made even where the contract does not specify for example that English law will govern. This demonstration of choice in the absence of a clear statement all depends on the facts in each case. These facts may be open to interpretation and thus uncertainty in the context of Internet transactions across borders and so specific legal advice must always be taken when a music business establishes its international website operations.

There are circumstances where this express choice of the law rules are varied.

Article 5 (2) of the Rome Convention makes clear that in certain circumstances, even though a choice of law is made by the parties to an online contract, a consumer may still benefit from the laws of their country of habitual residence. Since the Internet permits global transactions the effect of Article 5 is significant.

This overriding of the usual position applies for example if in that country the conclusion of the contract was preceded by a specific invitation addressed to the consumer or by advertising and the consumer in that country had taken all the steps necessary on their part for the conclusion of the contract.

This can cause problems with Internet contracts because a website may be regarded as a form of advertising. If a music website does not actually block viewers from specified countries as outlined above there is a risk that consumer protection laws may be introduced into a contract which the music business website operator never intended. The Rome Convention and also the Brussels

Regulation clearly protect consumers who contract with websites which make no attempt to exclude them.

CHECKLIST

- If the music business website is intended for access by an international audience, ensure the company understands the impact of the Brussels Regulation and Rome Convention.

- Review the music business website terms and conditions to ensure they fully address the question of sales of merchandise to European-based consumers.

Further Reading

Jonathan Cornthwaite, *The Internet and Intellectual Property*, 2nd edn, Monitor Press 2000, ISBN 1 871241871

Clive Gringras, *The Laws of the Internet*, 2nd edn, Butterworths 2002, ISBN 0406908087

Ann Harrison, *Music the Business – The Essential Guide to the Law and the Deals*, 2nd edn, Virgin Books 2003, ISBN 1852270136

Rex Nwakodo and Susan Singleton, *E-Contracts*, Tottel Publishing Ltd 2005, ISBN 1845929802

Andrew Sparrow, *The E-Commerce Handbook*, Fitzwarren Handbooks 2001, ISBN 0952481294

Andrew Sparrow, *The Law of Internet & Mobile Communications – The EU and US Contrasted*, TFM Publishing Ltd 2004, ISBN 1 903378184

Kolvin Stowe, 'Distance Selling Changes', *E-Commerce Law & Policy*, 7/8, August 2005

Index

About the Author

Andrew Sparrow is a national award-winning solicitor and founder of Lecote Solicitors, a niche commercial law firm concentrating on Internet, IT and new media law.

He was one of the first solicitors in the UK to pursue the legal issues relating to online business. Andrew is author of several books on commercial and Internet law published internationally.

In a national poll conducted in 2004 and supported by the Department of Trade and Industry he was acknowledged as one of 100 individuals in the UK who have contributed most to the development of the Internet in the last ten years.

He can be contacted at:

Lecote Solicitors
1 Victoria Square
Birmingham
B1 1BD
Tel: 0044 (0) 121 632 2285
Fax: 0044 (0) 121 632 2286
Email: Law@lecote.com
www.lecote.com

The HR Guide to European Mergers and Acquisitions
James F. Klein with Robert-Charles Kahn
0 566 08564 X

Integrated Intellectual Asset Management:
A Guide to Exploiting and Protecting Your
Organization's Intellectual Assets
Steve Manton
0 566 08721 9

Sources of Non-Official UK Statistics
Fifth Edition
Edited by David Mort
0 566 08449 X

Vetting and Monitoring Employees
Gillian Howard
0 566 08613 1

For further information on these and all our
titles visit our website – www.gowerpub.com
All online orders receive a discount

GOWER